PHOENIX

BRAD PRAGER

T0335278

CAMDEN HOUSE

First published 2019 by Camden House

Camden House is an imprint of Boydell & Brewer Inc.
668 Mt. Hope Avenue, Rochester, NY 14620, USA
www.camden-house.com
and of Boydell & Brewer Limited
PO Box 9, Woodbridge, Suffolk IP12 3DF, UK
www.boydellandbrewer.com

ISBN-13: 978-1-64014-038-7
ISBN-10: 1-64014-038-7

Library of Congress Cataloging-in-Publication Data

CIP data is available from the Library of Congress.

This publication is printed on acid-free paper.
Printed in the United States of America.

Phoenix

The opening scene of Christian Petzold's *Phoenix* (2014) contains a fleeting callback to Robert Siodmak's classic Hollywood film *The Killers* (1946). That famous shot—a road seen through the windshield of a moving car at night—heralds the arrival of two contract killers, and it has since become a cinematic stand-in for an imminent appointment with the executioner. According to Petzold, the deliberate resemblance between these films' first images was based on a suggestion by his friend and co-author Harun Farocki.[1] Their film, *Phoenix*, begins with Nelly Lenz, a German-Jewish singer, being driven toward the occupied city of Berlin in 1945 after having survived deportation to Auschwitz and being left for dead in the course of a death march.

Robert Siodmak, a German Jew who was born in Dresden, came to the United States in the 1930s. Denounced by Josef Goebbels, he fled the Nazis in 1933. Petzold is aware of the significance of Siodmak's work and has suggested that his plight as a persecuted German-Jewish exile, particularly later, upon his return to Germany, was a little like that of Nelly Lenz.[2] Petzold kept this in mind throughout the production of *Phoenix*. He recounts that when his film's star Nina Hoss remarked to him that her character Nelly lives "in the night, like a vampire," and observed that that the land around her is "a land of shadows," he concluded that *Phoenix* should be made in the style of film noir so that it would resonate with the work of filmmakers like Siodmak.[3]

After Nelly returns to Germany, her face badly scarred by a bullet wound, she has one thing on her mind: to reunite with Johnny, the German piano player to whom she was married when she was caught by the Gestapo and deported. Aided by her friend Lene Winter, Nelly undergoes plastic surgery, which successfully patches over her physical wounds, and she then goes in search of Johnny. Viewers may hope to see this onscreen couple, played by Nina Hoss and Ronald Zehrfeld, reunite, picking up where they left off as the two principal characters of Petzold's *Barbara* (2012), at the end of which they began to discover their feelings for one another, but when Nelly finally reconnects with Johnny she is thwarted: he does not recognize her. This failure on his part seems unlikely, but it is a calculated conceit on the screenwriters' part. Johnny's obliviousness comes from wanting neither to hear about the past, nor to see Nelly for who she now is; he prefers instead to entangle her in his plot to illicitly collect her own inheritance, one in which she—a woman he thinks resembles his wife—is asked to play the role of herself. Nelly would do anything to be back in Johnny's life again, so she agrees to his scheme, and, only in the film's denouement does she find her voice, confront him, and, in the process, take to task postwar Germany's unwillingness to acknowledge the Holocaust's survivors and victims.

In its formal characteristics *Phoenix* seems to draw many of its motifs from major works of film noir, and Petzold has made clear that this was his intention.[4] The film is set in 1945 and derives period-appropriate mise-en-scène and atmosphere from that era's masterworks. But for German filmmakers to borrow from that period, as do Petzold and Farocki when they appropriate from *The Killers*, means more than merely duplicating its fashionable clothing and hairstyles; the atmosphere they import into *Phoenix* calls to mind the historical and psychological perspectives of a particular set of émigrés. Some scholars prefer to describe this same set of films not with reference to film noir, but rather with reference to the condition of exile, drawing on Theodor Adorno's description of expatriates as persons forced to contend with the damage ensuing from their estrangement, and with the burden of living in environments that feel alien to them.[5]

Many of the most celebrated directors associated with that era, Jews who came to the United States just before the Holocaust, including émigrés such as Billy Wilder, Ernst Lubitsch, and Siodmak, can be understood as the conveyors of an exported legacy of German film. It would, of course, be unreasonable to group the overwhelming contribution émigrés made to Hollywood in the decades after the introduction of sound film under any single label, but Gerd Gemünden asserts that among the "hundreds of German-speaking film professionals who lived and worked in Hollywood during the mid-1920s and after," the majority "were Jewish refugees who escaped the threat of the Nazi death camps."[6] Hollywood was, for them, a fertile creative ground. Lutz Koepnick speculates that Siodmak grafted his personal experience of "forced displacement," or "the exile's lack of authorship over his own narrative of life" onto his films.[7] Works by exiled filmmakers frequently distinguish themselves owing to recurring motifs such as misrecognition, the loss of identity, and other comparable hallmarks connected with their estranged viewpoints. *Phoenix* frequently calls to mind Siodmak's major works, including *The Phantom Lady* (1944) and *The Dark Mirror* (1946), films that were known to Petzold and Farocki, and which they had discussed with one another.[8]

It is certainly the case that Petzold and Farocki deliberately introduced motifs from exile films of the 1940s into *Phoenix*, but it is also possible that their choice of subject made these inclusions inevitable—that is, that their premise brought with it a patently German-Jewish history. Would it have been possible to make a film about a German Jew returning to Berlin from Auschwitz in 1945 without calling to mind the work and experiences of émigré filmmakers? It seems unlikely that one could touch on this topic without referring, at least tangentially, to the interrupted lives of figures such as Siodmak, or to emigrated artists who had once made Berlin their home, like the musician Kurt Weill or the actor Peter Lorre. Nelly Lenz, the protagonist of *Phoenix*, is a professional singer who comes back to Berlin to reconstruct her life and wants everything to be exactly as it was before the war. In telling the story of Nelly's postwar odyssey—her return, wounded and scarred, from the inferno of a concentration camp—the film's director, its screenwriters, and its principals each undertake to assemble the pieces of a broken tradition, creating continuity where real German-Jewish narratives were fragmentary and filled with gaps. They thus find themselves ventriloquizing Jewish voices. In one interview, Petzold explains that he and Farocki came upon the idea that Nelly and her ex-husband Johnny, as a singer and pianist in a mixed marriage, should draw on the model of Lotte Lenya and Kurt Weill.[9]

None of the film's filmmakers, neither Petzold nor Farocki nor Nina Hoss, are themselves Jewish, but they took steps to steep *Phoenix* in German-Jewish heritage; Petzold and Farocki find inspiration in the films of Robert Siodmak and those of his brother Curt; Nina Hoss's performance looks to that of artists such as Lorre and Weill (not to mention that of a few non-Jewish émigrés like Hedy Lamarr); and Nina Kunzendorf's character, Lene, a Jewish aid worker who openly expresses resentment toward Germany, expresses the ideas of emigrated thinkers such as Hannah Arendt and the Austrian survivor Jean Améry. Throughout *Phoenix*, voices of German and German-speaking Jews are directly and indirectly introduced, and in this way the film becomes a kind of séance. In calling back to Siodmak's *The Killers*, to Lorre's performance as an émigré in *The Face Behind the Mask* (1941), and even by way of its multiple inclusions of Kurt Weill's song "Speak Low," *Phoenix* draws on many sources, building a bridge out of ruins; the film is a reassembly of moments drawn from the heritage of German-Jewish culture and filmmaking, a meta-diegetic universe that picks up the threads of a violently interrupted tradition.

Although many films share overlapping imagery, and any two films may abide comparison, Petzold, throughout his oeuvre, intentionally draws on a wide range of cinematic sources. One of his earliest films, *Cuba Libre* (1996), for example, frequently and deliberately refers back to Edgar Ulmer's 1945 film noir *Detour*, and his *Jerichow* (2008), which was a more-than-loose adaptation of James M. Cain's 1934 novel *The Postman Always Rings Twice*, expects viewers to look back at the novel's 1946 and 1981 film adaptations as well as at *Ossessione*, Luchino Visconti's Italian version from 1943, to which Petzold often refers. *Jerichow* not only changes the identity of the novel's Greek husband, identifying him as a man of Turkish descent; the film also includes multiple evocations of Rainer Werner Fassbinder's *The Merchant of Four Seasons* (1971) and *Ali: Fear Eats the Soul* (1973).[10] *Jerichow* is exemplary for the director's technique of isolating elements from earlier works and situating them in new contexts. Each of these elements serves as a focal point, presenting itself as an instance of refraction. It would be impossible to adapt a book from 1934 or reproduce, however freely or unfaithfully, a sequence from a 1946 film without commenting on what has changed in the intervening years. The many layers of *Phoenix*—the film's numerous instances of refraction—include 1945, which is when the film is set, when the concentration and death camps were liberated, and when many German-Jewish exile films were produced in Hollywood, as well as the early to mid-1960s, which was the time of the Auschwitz trials in Germany, the time frame in which Hubert Monteilhet's novel *Return from the Ashes* (*Le retour des cendres*, 1961), the source of the screenplay for *Phoenix*, was published, and also the time during which French Holocaust memorial culture was shaped by the reception of Alain Resnais and Jean Cayrol's *Night and Fog* (1955). The film's temporal layers also include 2014, which was the year *Phoenix* was produced and the moment at which Petzold and Farocki decided to intervene in German film's unfinished dialogue with the Nazi past. Their film's many stations reframe and expose one another. They are the prisms through which the language and images of *Phoenix* are mediated, each frame and composition bending and shaping our perspective on those that came before.

A year after Hubert Monteilhet's *Return from the Ashes* first appeared, it was published in Yvonne de Hair's German translation. Petzold read Monteilhet's novel in German and claims not to have been familiar with J. Lee Thompson's 1965 British film adaptation, which starred Ingrid Thulin and Maximilian Schell.[11] Although Monteilhet's novel could indeed be described as thrilling, it is hardly a clumsy potboiler; it works outward from the conceit that the main character is already dead and that we are reading her diary. It thus features subjective narration, which forces us to wonder whether the information with which we are provided is wholly reliable. Beyond that, it touches on a number of difficult themes, including the guilt and shame experienced by a Holocaust survivor, and the uneasy re-integration of Jews into French culture after the war. *Phoenix* draws much from Monteilhet's book and retains several major details: beyond essential elements of the premise, some exchanges are closely reproduced, and, insofar as "Nelly" is, according to some, an accepted sobriquet for Elizabeth, Petzold and Farocki even retained Elizabeth Wolf as their main character's name. (It is revealed, in the course of *Phoenix*, that Nelly Lenz's maiden name was "Wolff"). But Petzold and Farocki also introduce many changes: they move the setting from Paris to Berlin; the Holocaust survivor, who is said to be returning from Auschwitz rather than Dachau, is no longer a doctor but rather a singer; and the character of the ex-husband, who in the novel is named Stanislas Pilgrin, is turned into a musician instead of an expert chess player. The source material is thus reconfigured in a way that expresses as much about the interests of the filmmakers as it does about the original text; it is a transformation rather than a straightforward adaptation, and much has been gained by displacing Monteilhet's narrative from France to Germany. Postwar Germany was beset by an entirely different raft of concerns from postwar

France, and that was precisely the filmmakers' point: as a Jew, Nelly was an unwelcome returnee in Germany, and few Germans wanted to hear a tale told by, in the words of her ex-husband Johnny, a "ragged camp internee" (*eine zerstörte Lagerinsassin*). In the German context, Johnny's belief-beggaring obtuseness stands out as representative of a wider national reluctance to confront the past.

Farocki was responsible for drawing Petzold's attention to Monteilhet's novel. Although credit for a film's authorship is traditionally given to the director, the collaboration between these two filmmakers is somewhat exceptional, and, based on Petzold's own accounts, it seems that his films—nearly every one of the fourteen or so films he made prior to 2014—would have been measurably different had it not been for Farocki's participation. A prolific documentarian and director of essay films, Farocki was Petzold's most influential teacher at the film school from which he graduated, the Deutsche Film- und Fernsehakademie Berlin (the DFFB).[12] Around the time Petzold made his first feature-length film, *Pilots* (1995), Farocki, with whom he consulted on the screenplay, became less Petzold's teacher than his constant collaborator.[13] It was the start of a two-decade-long working relationship wherein Farocki was credited on nearly every one of Petzold's films, either for dramaturgy, for "consultation," or, quite frequently, as the screenplay's co-author. Their working relationship, as Petzold describes it retrospectively, mirrored the idealized intellectual friendships characteristic of the German Romantics. When Petzold describes how productive it was to work through ideas with Farocki, he refers to Heinrich von Kleist's famous text "On the Gradual Completion of Thoughts During Speech" (1807).[14] Although Kleist's essay is ironic about the gap between thought and expression and takes issue with the common conviction that thoughts have existence prior to their articulation, Petzold, in referring to Kleist, is asserting that his ideas found their finest form when he was in Farocki's presence. Their long tradition of collaboration is a story of mutual inspiration in which they would aid one another in seeing their visions through to completion. While Petzold was pleased to have Farocki add to and revise his screenplays, it seems that Farocki was equally pleased to have Petzold, with *Phoenix*, adopt and improve on themes he developed in his own narrative feature *Betrayed* (*Betrogen*, 1985). Many of the ideas for *Phoenix*, especially the film's deliberate allusions to the work of Peter Lorre and to Alfred Hitchcock's *Vertigo* (1958), came as suggestions from Farocki, who died unexpectedly in the summer of 2014 and did not live to see their film's final cut.[15]

In light of the timing of Farocki's death, it may come as a surprise that *Phoenix* is not dedicated to him. Petzold's subsequent film, *Transit* (2018), is dedicated to Farocki, and that dedication appears in the film's opening titles, just before the first image is seen on screen. The dedication of *Phoenix*, however, comes right before the film's end credits. In keeping with its emphasis on German-Jewish history and experience, Petzold dedicated it to Fritz Bauer, the German-Jewish prosecutor who was a driving force behind Germany's Auschwitz trials in the early and mid-1960s. Bauer remains mostly unknown to many of the film's Anglophone viewers. He was born in Stuttgart in 1903, and became a district court judge at a relatively young age, but he was removed from his position when the Nazis came to power in 1933 and was imprisoned for some months in Camp Heuberg, one of the first German concentration camps. Bauer escaped to Denmark in 1936 and only survived by making his way to Sweden in 1943. In 1949 he returned to West Germany, eventually becoming attorney general for the state of Hesse. Bauer is thus not only an émigré but also a returnee, and, in this narrow sense, his story intersects with that of Nelly Lenz. As a prosecutor, he was better positioned than most to remind Germany of the wounds it had left on its surviving Jews and the stain it had inflicted on its own history. Bauer seems to have felt that his survival came with the obligation to remind Germans that they were not finished with the past. Several recent German films, including *The People vs. Fritz Bauer* (*Der Staat gegen*

Fritz Bauer, 2015) and the television film *The General Case* (*Die Akte General*, 2015), have tried to dramatize Bauer's role in initiating the Frankfurt Auschwitz trials, and *Phoenix*, in its treatment of Germans' unwillingness to confront elements of their own past, contrasts sharply with the most prominent contemporary film about the Auschwitz trials, Giulio Ricciarelli's *Labyrinth of Lies* (*Im Labyrinth des Schweigens*, 2014). In attempting to appeal to its German audiences, that film all but erases Bauer's importance.[16] Ricciarelli prefers to center his narrative on a fictionalized non-Jewish German prosecutor, who acts as the prosecution's sole advocate.

Many of the Jews who were still in Germany after the war were immigrants and displaced persons who managed to survive in eastern Europe and were forcibly marched into Germany. Many were, unlike Nelly Lenz, biding time in German camps, hoping to make their way to America, England, or Palestine. Bauer, by contrast, when he returned to Germany, intended to stay. His self-understanding as a German was vexed in a way that corresponds to the motifs of *Phoenix*: it is by no means clear that Petzold's protagonist, who hopes to make her home in Germany, identifies as a Jew—as a matter of fact, she makes it clear that she does not. Prior to her deportation, her self-image was evidently the same as any other non-Jewish German. Bauer, for his part, understood that one could surely see one's self in those terms, but he also felt compelled to reproach Germany for its failings. He thus found himself in the position of provocateur, and, to some, his very existence as a returned Jew, much like Nelly, the "ragged camp internee," was nothing other than a distressing reminder of a wound.[17] But Bauer maintained a strong affinity for German culture and ideas, and he considered those ideas to be a part of his own heritage. In an interview in Erwin Leiser's documentary *Murder by Signature* (*Eichmann und das dritte Reich*, 1961) Bauer explains that Germany is proud of Goethe, and proud of its economic miracle, but that it must also own up to being the homeland of Eichmann and the many who helped him. He sums up the matter: "as each day consists of both day and night, the history of every people has its light and its shadowy sides." Insofar as Bauer's life, work, and complicated relationship to Germany intersect with the story of Nelly's return, it is clear why Petzold dedicated *Phoenix* to him.

Nelly's Homecoming

The German word for a "return home" is *Heimkehr*. After having been deported to Auschwitz, Nelly comes back to Berlin as a *Heimkehrerin* (that word's feminine form). In German cinema, *Heimkehr* carries with it a distinctive history tied to the First and Second World Wars. Joe May's Weimar-era film *Heimkehr* (1928) depicts a World War I German soldier who assumes that his friend and comrade has died while escaping a forced labor camp. He then returns to Germany and falls in love with his comrade's fiancé, but his friend eventually makes his way home to find that he has survived the war and narrowly dodged death only to experience a hurtful betrayal. May's *Heimkehr* centered on how the First World War unsettled its soldiers' personal lives. A more disquieting film, certainly in retrospect, with that same title was made during the Second World War: Gustav Ucicky's 1941 Nazi film *Heimkehr*, which was produced under Goebbels's oversight. That film concentrated mainly on a group of ethnic Germans who want to return home ("heim ins Reich"), as they confront a series of exclusions, discriminations, and persecutions in a fictive Poland of the 1930s. The persecution they suffer presages that of the Jews in Germany, and the film served as an incitement in an ongoing war, a rationalization of Germany's belligerence.

Phoenix's premise might also remind viewers of the story of Martin Guerre, the sixteenth-century Frenchman who is well known in cinema because of Daniel Vigne's *The Return of Martin Guerre* (1982). Guerre was thought to have abandoned his village in the Pyrenees until, years later, an imposter returned claiming to be him. Guerre's wife, according to the story, chose to take up with the imposter. She preferred the easy answers he provided, which presented her with an opportunity to forget the knotty circumstances attached to her real husband's disappearance. Nelly's story shares some elements in common with Guerre's: she has returned home changed by what she has been through. She left Germany involuntarily but comes back a different woman, and the ex-husband to whom she returns prefers to interact with another version of her rather than confront the complexities associated with the recent past.

According to Marco Abel, all of Petzold's films are about "people who either try to figure out how to escape Germany, are forced to return to it, or desire to carve out a space for themselves [in it]," regardless of whether Germany wants them to.[18] In an interview, Petzold adds that most great stories are essentially "travel narratives," and that "such narratives only pretend that people set out on a journey into the foreign."[19] He continues, "in the end, it's all a version of Homer's *Odyssey*: mostly, such narratives are about getting home."[20] Odysseus, literature's best-known *Heimkehrer*, is the archetypal returnee: he sets out for Troy and eventually returns to Ithaca following a long and perilous series of struggles, as well as a journey to the underworld. Fighting in a war—and not only a war, but also a visit to Hades, a *katabasis*—transforms Odysseus, and he is only recognized at home thanks to a scar he acquired before his departure. The man who set out for Troy is not the one who returns. Although the emphases differ, the classical gesture remains the same, and *Phoenix* accentuates one of the essential corollaries to Homer's premise: not only has Nelly, the returnee, changed, but the nation and the people who knew her seem to have changed accordingly. She discovers that some Germans would prefer not to see her and that she, reciprocally, can no longer see Germany the same way. Writing of German drama's longstanding proclivity for Odysseus narratives, the philologist Walter Jens summarizes, "As shadows, ghosts released from the realm of the dead, [travelers] return to a world whose signs they no longer understand. No Penelope, no faithful Eumaeus, and no son awaits them; their parents are dead or have turned their backs on them, their wives have become alien, and everything that greets them, those envoys returning from hell into the light, is disconcerting and uncanny."[21] For the survivor, a return home, a journey "from hell into the light," is a voyage into an alien land.

Phoenix inscribes itself into a long literary tradition, one that reaches as far back as Homer, but, as indicated, Petzold's work frequently takes its cues from other films. Many of its themes have appeared on screen before—not least in May's *Heimkehr* and in Vigne's *The Return of Martin Guerre*—but in its formal characteristics *Phoenix* culls many motifs from films generally considered to be films noir. To choose only one example from the 1940s films on which *Phoenix* plays, one can look at Robert Siodmak's *The Dark Mirror*. In that film, Olivia de Havilland plays her own doppelgänger. She is cast as twin sisters, one of whom gaslights the other; she is a bad sister trying to make a good one go mad. *Phoenix* can be described similarly insofar as it thematizes Nelly's fragmented identity: on the one hand, she wants to remain Johnny Lenz's wife, and even though Johnny prefers to believe she is deceased, she wants nothing more than to reunite with him. On the other hand, she is a traumatized Holocaust survivor for whom everything has changed. Like Odysseus returning from the underworld, what was once familiar now seems far away and strange, and she is urged by Lene to respond to her feelings of anomie, to identify less as a German and more as a Jew, and to relocate to Palestine. Nelly returns to Berlin in the hope of becoming, once again, Johnny's wife, but her postwar experiences gradually bring her around to Lene's point of view.

In the film's mesmerizing first few minutes Petzold and Farocki introduce the image of Nelly's fully bandaged face, a hallmark of horror films, into *Phoenix*'s storyline. Neither Monteilhet's *Return from the Ashes* nor Thompson's 1965 adaptation of Monteilhet's novel pay much attention to the details of the protagonist's surgery, and in neither one does the Holocaust survivor's bandaged head play a prominent role. This imagery calls to mind the Invisible Man, who first appeared in an eponymous film in 1933 and again in 1940 in *The Invisible Man Returns*, a film written by Robert Siodmak's émigré brother Curt, as well as in Edwin Marin's *Invisible Agent* from 1941, which was also written by Curt Siodmak.[22] The most instructive Invisible Man intertext, however, is the 1944 film *The Invisible Man's Revenge*, in which the translucent main character, who was left for dead by his fellow explorers in the African wild, vengefully exacts retribution. The horrifying element in each of these films is the anxiety—shared by the protagonist and the audience—that there might be nothing beneath the bandages. Scars and wounds can be horrifying to look at, but when invisible men go mad, it is usually because of the instability of their egos. Psychosis is a stock motif in these films, in which formerly secure identities evaporate. If bandaged protagonists cannot see their own faces, then they lack the anchor that keeps their drives and fears in check. The prospect of being faceless is less liberating than it is maddening, and the most formidable source of fear is the existential abyss that opens beneath invisible men, whose best hope of holding onto their sanity lies in restoring their visibility.

The evaporation of Nelly's sense of identity, one of the central themes of *Phoenix*, calls to mind that same abyss, and it stands to reason that the film's first spoken line is a call for an identity check: an English-speaking American soldier at the border asks to see Nelly and Lene's passports. Petzold does not make clear whether Nelly is in possession of the proper papers, but given the circumstances it is highly improbable that she would have retained her German documents, and it is also unlikely that she possesses a recent photo of her face. There would be, in any case, nothing to compare the photo with—her face has been mangled and she keeps it completely concealed. Lene responds to the request by making vague allusions

The first glimpse of Nelly's fully bandaged face.

to Nelly's recent past, explaining that she comes "from the camps," but these attempts to skirt the soldier's demands are unpersuasive. In her bid to dissuade him, she also interjects, "C'mon, she's not Eva Braun." The offhand remark, it turns out, is a cryptic comment on the film itself: in one interview Petzold slipped, accidentally conflating Eva Braun with Fassbinder's famous heroine Maria Braun. When asked about how other German films dealing with the Second World War and the Holocaust inspired the production of *Phoenix*, Petzold replied, "I thought about Fassbinder, when he made his period pictures like *The Marriage of Eva Braun*—I mean *Maria Braun*!"[23] Played by Hanna Schygulla in Fassbinder's 1979 film, Maria Braun remains one of New German Cinema's most iconic figures. She married a German soldier late in the war, and, when he failed to return home, she began building a new life. Fassbinder's *Marriage of Maria Braun* could likewise have been entitled "Phoenix."

Petzold admires Fassbinder, a groundbreaking director with an unparalleled talent for integrating into his work compositions and themes from directors such as Hitchcock and Douglas Sirk, among others, as well as countless generic tropes from melodrama, film noir, and even science fiction.[24] But if Petzold is inspired by Fassbinder's appropriations, he must be seeing his predecessor's work through a bifocal lens: on the one hand, like Petzold, Fassbinder knew how to undercut, refigure, and rework traditions in order to comment on German history and on German film's hot and cold affair with Hollywood. The two directors' agendas are, in that respect, similar. On the other hand, as revolutionary as Fassbinder's film was, *The Marriage of Maria Braun* is inscribed into a film history that has, for the most part, marginalized Jewish stories. The film was radical when it was released because it re-examined the conditions that led to Germany's economic miracle and because it was provocative about the war's lingering ideological aftereffects, not because it convincingly demonstrated any interest in working through the Holocaust. German-Jewish survivors experienced the so-called *Stunde Null*, the zero hour at the war's conclusion when what remained of Germany declared an end to the Nazi racial state, differently from non-Jewish Germans, and Jews' experiences have less often been recounted. In this sense, the soldier's terse dismissal of Lene's comment may be taken as an oblique indication on the part of the screenwriters that German film has had enough of stories centered on characters such as Maria Braun. In this sense, *Phoenix* is a critique of that tradition's emphasis on the fates of non-Jewish victims in light of the excluded and forgotten perspectives on that same past.

Audience members' curiosities may, at this early point in the film, be awakened about the extent of Nelly's wounds, and when the American soldier bluntly insists, "I wanna see her face!" he may be speaking on behalf of the spectators. Nelly is unable to utter any words of protest, and the sounds of her heavy breathing substitute for her otherwise absent voice. She proceeds to gradually unwrap her bandages, and the camera teases an unveiling before it cuts away, choosing instead to register the impression Nelly's face makes on the soldier.[25] His reaction provides us with information about her wounds: his gaze sinks, he seems remorseful, and he murmurs a subdued apology. Petzold declines to indulge our voyeuristic curiosity, and this conscious decision against revealing her appearance may be carried over from prohibitions on images of Holocaust violence.[26] This choice, however, also has the peculiar effect of amplifying Nelly's mortification. The Auschwitz survivor Primo Levi more than once set out to describe Holocaust survivors' sense of shame. Levi, who had been left for dead by the perpetrators at Auschwitz shortly before that camp's liberation, summed up his feelings: "Coming out of the darkness, one suffered because of the reacquired consciousness of having been diminished. Not by our will, cowardice, or fault, yet nevertheless we had lived for months and years at an animal level [. . .]. [A]ny space for reflection, reasoning, experiencing emotions was wiped out."[27] Nelly appears to have endured a similar diminishment, and shame was built into her character's backstory from the beginning: in *Return from the Ashes*, Monteilhet's Elizabeth Wolf was said to have engaged in sex work in order to survive Dachau. Having been forced into sexual subservience heightens the character's humiliation, and she feels she has to conceal that part of her story when she returns. In adding this detail, Monteilhet was responding to the need to more thoroughly explain his character's shame, but he was also trading on a lurid fantasy that was, at the time, attached to many Holocaust survivors. Petzold and Farocki, with good reason, chose not to include this in their screenplay.

As though it were not enough of a burden that Nelly is scarred to the point of near unrecognizability, she is also returning home to an unwelcoming nation. She identifies as a German and thus likely shares a measure of anxiety about her nation's military occupation, but as a Jew, her postwar presence in Germany is a source of bewilderment. A large percentage of the Jews residing in Germany after the war were eastern Europeans who were living in displaced persons camps.[28] Unpleasantly enough, those were sites such as the former camps of Buchenwald and Belsen, which had now been altered to suit new purposes. The people housed there did not want to return to eastern Europe, where pogroms may have awaited them, and they instead awaited the opportunity to emigrate to Palestine

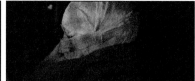

Nelly starts to unwrap her bandages.

and other locations. Many of the remaining Jews, the one in five who were not in camps and who returned to German society, were made aware that it was, in Attina Grossmann's words, "not the dead six million [...] who agitated resentful Germans, but the handful who were still present."[29] In the summer of 1945 fewer than 7,000 Jews resided in Berlin, and less than twenty percent of those were returnees from concentration camps.[30] Nelly's journey to the camps and back might seem representative to some viewers, but it actually corresponds to the experience of a relatively small subset of survivors. As someone burdened with a double identity—at once a German in fear of the occupation and a scarred, unwelcome German-Jewish Holocaust survivor—Nelly now crosses the bridge, bound for what was once her home.

The bridge seen at the beginning of *Phoenix* separates two geographical locations, and it also separates Nelly's two states of being. She was a prisoner in the East—at Auschwitz, at least for a time—and she is now about to become a Holocaust survivor in Berlin; she will thus awaken on an entirely different shore. As in Greek mythology, in which Charon ferries passengers across the river, the bridge in this scene is a conduit between death and life. Returns to life, however, can be double-edged; the dead are frequently unwelcome among the living and new circumstances are never exactly as they were. Nelly's ex-husband presumes she is dead, and based on the limited information we have, her tormentors had left her for dead. In this sense, her return to Germany is, for those who receive her, a resurrection. In Monteilhet's novel, Elizabeth

Wolf identifies her condition with that of the resurrected Lazarus. She feels that she needs more time to regain her equilibrium before seeing her husband, because she is "like Lazarus coming out of the tomb."[31] This association, drawing on the New Testament, would be a curious one for a Jewish survivor to make; and it is one that might occur more readily to Christians. In the 1958 preface to Elie Wiesel's *Night*, for example, the French Catholic novelist and dramatist François Mauriac compares Wiesel to Lazarus, writing that the author of *Night* had "the gaze of a Lazarus risen from the dead yet still held captive in the somber regions into which he had strayed, stumbling over desecrated corpses."[32] Wiesel had returned from the camps, but, according to Mauriac, he still belonged to the world of the dead; he was a Lazarus not yet reborn.

Not long after Monteilhet wrote *Return from the Ashes* and used the Holocaust as a backdrop for his page-turner, the American poet Sylvia Plath wrote the poem "Lady Lazarus" (1962), which prominently featured the image of a female Holocaust victim rising from the dead. The persona in Plath's poem dies several deaths, possibly suicides, as a result of men's viciousness. She describes her reincarnated skin as being as bright as a Nazi lampshade; she "melts to a shriek" and "turn[s] and burn[s]." Plath's Lady Lazarus has red hair and ascends from "out of the ash" to "eat men like air." Her reincarnated figure is wrathful, and she is resentful of the men who bury her again and again, but she is powerful because her death stands alongside that of others. The poem's persona is a woman speaking in solidarity with other women; she adopts the rhetoric of repeated deaths in order to speak for many survivors, and for that reason, her death is more than only her own. She is a female survivor who returns from the dead, refusing to be forgotten. In this way, the figures of Lazarus and the Phoenix overlap, each one having seen the other side and returned.

Petzold has said many times that he absolutely did not intend for Nelly to be understood as the titular Phoenix, preferring to think of Germany or even the city of Berlin as that which, in his film, attempts to rise from its charred remains.[33] Moreover, it can hardly be said that Nelly, shattered by her experiences, returns to Berlin in possession of an extraordinary, supernatural power; if she is a Phoenix, she remains steeped in ashes, burdened by the memory of the forsaken dead. The only reference to the Phoenix in Monteilhet's novel emphasizes something entirely different from fiery rebirth. As Elizabeth Wolf reflects on her devotion to Stanislas, the character on whom Johnny is based, she observes, "I know that I made a Phoenix out of this cuckoo, but I needed him to survive."[34] Though Nelly herself could be understood in terms of the figure of the Phoenix, one who awakens with a debt to those who were left behind, and who may eventually avenge herself on her perpetrators, the film's Phoenix may be an altogether different breed of bird. Following from the passage in *Return from the Ashes*, the Phoenix imagery may be applied to Johnny, Nelly's bright source of hope. Heading "home" over the bridge is a step in the journey toward what she imagines to be Johnny's redemptive luminescence. When the film's opening scene finally fades to white—or fades to a bright light—as Nelly and Lene cross the bridge, it is because Nelly is now headed back to Johnny, a cuckoo she erroneously believes possesses the properties of a Phoenix.

When we encounter Nelly awaiting surgery in the clinic, she is lying beneath a framed print of *Angelus Novus*, the 1920 painting by the Swiss-German artist Paul Klee. Klee's painting has taken on added importance among his works owing to the role it plays in Benjamin's 1940 essay "Theses on the Philosophy of History." Benjamin, who, while fleeing from the Nazis and attempting to emigrate, committed suicide, interpreted the lone figure depicted in the work as similar to the image in his mind of the angel of history, a winged observer of a mortal storm, helpless to do anything to halt the ceaseless accumulation of human debris at its feet.[35] Klee's Angel, the Angelus Novus, is not the angel of history, nor was Benjamin

The opening sequence concludes with a bright light.

intending to describe Klee's painting; he was instead declaring that this is how the angel of history might look. That angel, he writes, wants to awaken the dead, and, in the face of tragedy, "make whole what has been smashed."[36] If the Phoenix is imagined to have been among the dead and to have returned to the world bearing their memories and burdened by their misfortunes, then this angel, consistent with Benjamin's messianic philosophy of history, can be seen as a Jewish counterpart to the Greek mythological image.

If this purposefully chosen element of mise-en-scène may be taken to reflect Nelly's present state, then it does so only insofar as Klee's expressionist distortions—the angel's hair in tangles, its face seemingly fragmented into sections—reflect how Nelly perceives her shattered physiognomy. In this same scene, Nelly learns that most of the Jews she knew and loved have been murdered. Lene delivers the news bluntly—"your entire family is dead"—and she seems to deliberately refuse to recognize that Nelly might also consider Johnny to be a member of her family. Nelly eventually comes to terms with the logic of Lene's perspective, and the painting's appearance in the film foreshadows what she will become: a survivor who chooses not to turn her back on those who died.

The surgical clinic's techniques may at first glance seem anachronistic, but maxillofacial surgery including cosmetic facial surgery had already been popularized following the First World War as a treatment for soldiers who were disfigured. It is surely plausible that this operation would have been performed on a survivor, and the procedure's details remind us that Holocaust survivors were also among the war's wounded; Nelly was shot in the face, and, based on what we see of her surgeon's sketch, she resembles a disfigured soldier in a painting by Otto Dix. As Lene makes us aware, Nelly is in the unusual position of being able to afford the procedure's expense. There is no historical basis for what happens here—Monteilhet's novel neither claims to be based on a true story, nor was there a

Nelly lies beneath Paul Klee's *Angelus Novus.*

real Elizabeth Wolf—but the surgical conceit provides a convenient metaphor for a situation wherein events have shattered the core of a survivor's ore-war identity. Nelly's aspiration to reacquire the face she once had is a literalization of her longing to reset her existence. However, the premise that Nelly's face is a blank surface onto which a brighter future may be written is complicated because new surfaces never completely erase original ones. New faces never come without fetters; people and their features each bring with them a past.[37]

In response to the plastic surgeon's ostensibly routine series of questions, Nelly can only grunt, for the most part leaving Lene to speak for her. The doctor asks, "you came back here [to Germany] as a Jewess, why?" and the question is hardly rhetorical insofar as it is one of the central ones that *Phoenix* aims to answer. To this question, neither Nelly nor Lene has a response. The two of them later engage in a consultation with the doctor about Nelly's hopes for her appearance. Speaking through bandages she asserts, "I want to look exactly as before," and the doctor informs her that this is unlikely. Attempts to remake old faces, he explains, never come out right, and, he adds, it is generally an advantage to find one's self with a new face. Both of these arguments bespeak the difficulties connected with Nelly's re-integration; no one ever starts from scratch. The doctor encourages Nelly to embrace her new features and matter-of-factly offers her choices: he could rebuild her face so that she resembles Zarah Leander, the diva who, despite her efforts to steer away from politics, became a mega-star in the Nazi film industry, or alternately the actress Kristina Söderbaum, whose popularity also peaked during that period. The doctor's proposals come with only the feeblest acknowledgment that Leander and Söderbaum have "fallen out of fashion," a euphemistic way of conceding that their association with the Third Reich tainted them, particularly Söderbaum, who was married to Veit Harlan, the propagandist responsible for the virulently anti-Semitic *Jud Süss* (1940). Ironically, both of the doctor's examples of "new faces" are old faces. Their conversation reveals that neither "new" nor "exactly as before" are viable options. On this point, both the doctor and his patient are misguided.

The conversation at the clinic has a precedent in Monteilhet's novel. The exchange between Elizabeth Wolf and her doctor, which to some extent served as a basis for this one, centers on the protagonist's desire to assert her Judaism. As Wolf begins the process of having her scars repaired, her doctor offers her "a nose made to order" and encourages her to opt for a "truly Parisian nose."[38] After she asks whether she can instead be given a Jewish one, the doctor grasps what she is trying to tell him: she sees herself as Jewish and intends to continue doing so. Wolf summarizes her postwar feelings: "I'd almost forgotten that I was Jewish. Then I was reminded of the fact very harshly. I must keep hold of that reminder."[39] Monteilhet's character, in contrast with Nelly, is adamant that she means to remain a Jew, and the changes made in Petzold and Farocki's version highlight the purposes for which their screenplay retooled the novel. If something is gained in displacing the story's setting to Germany, it is that *Phoenix* addresses the futility, in that context, of dreaming that one might again become what one was. Before the war, Nelly identified as a German more than as a German Jew, and she is, at this point, not particularly concerned with attempting to look Jewish, whatever that might mean. She is only interested in re-establishing the life that was taken from her.

The ruination of a face and its ensuing replacement are key plot points in Robert Florey's suspenseful American film *The Face Behind the Mask* (1941), which was well known to Petzold and Farocki. In Florey's film, the Hungarian-born Jewish actor Peter Lorre plays Janos Szabo, a Hungarian émigré and trained watchmaker who arrives in New York on a boat hoping to start a new life and eventually bring over the woman he plans to marry. Shortly after his arrival, he is badly burned in a hotel fire. Following his convalescence, during which his head is entirely wrapped in bandages, he is left with few options; surgery is too expensive and painstaking, so he chooses to conceal his unsightly scars with an off-putting synthetic mask. The film's opening titles allude to the fact that Lorre's character might be a Jewish émigré, although that is never made explicit. Lorre rarely played roles that were overtly Jewish, but when Jewish actors appeared on German screens in the 1930s, the Nazis tended to treat their performances as unmediated (and nonfictional) glimpses into Jewish lives.[40] Unsurprisingly, their judgments had been harsh against Lorre, who had played his share of outsiders and eccentrics, most notably a child murderer in Fritz Lang's *M* (1931), a performance upon which anti-Semites were quick to seize. Many feel, however, that Florey's *The Face Behind the Mask* approximated elements of Lorre's own biography insofar as it is an emigration story that can be seen to allegorize the actor's wartime flight from Europe. Szabo, the character played by Lorre, is physically wounded, even defaced, in the act of emigration; he becomes a new man who only vaguely resembles the person he once was, and his mask is clearly more than merely superficial.

Farocki used footage from Florey's 1941 film as the starting point for a film of his own entitled *The Double Face of Peter Lorre* (*Das doppelte Gesicht—Peter Lorre*, 1984), which centered on the damaging impact that the war and forced emigration had on Lorre's health and on his body of work.[41] Farocki's film depicts Lorre as an actor who ended up feeling that even his private face had taken on the qualities of a mask; it centers on the consequences of Lorre's flight from Germany after the Nazis made their first arrests in the film industry. Like Siodmak, Lorre, who was born László Löwenstein, fled Germany in 1933. He headed first to France and, ultimately, to Hollywood. He eventually grew tired of making the faces Hollywood wanted him to make, and in this way *The Face Behind the Mask* tells the story of his loss of identity and of his ever-narrower prospects for self-expression. Lorre felt reduced to his conspicuously wide eyes and accented speech. In Farocki's account, the actor finally resigned himself to doing clumsy burlesques and died too young, prior to his sixtieth birthday.

That Petzold wrote an essay of his own about *The Face Behind the Mask* probably owes itself equally to his interests in Lorre's compelling biography and in Farocki's cinephilic tastes.[42] In that essay, Petzold makes the typical assumption that Lorre's character is Jewish, but he also makes a number of incisive formal observations. His short analysis of the film dwells at length on the scenes set in surgical clinics: one in which Lorre first sees his own damaged face in the mirror, and another in which he learns that the doctor is not going to be able to restore his looks and that he is going to have to live behind a mask. The 1941 film clearly had an impact on *Phoenix*. The shot, for example, in which the soldier encounters Nelly's unbandaged face recalls Florey's depiction of the nurse who first lays eyes on Szabo after he has been burned. If the more general parallels weren't clear enough—that the two stories each deal with émigrés forced from their homes, ones who are disfigured and fated to endure the reconstruction of their faces—Petzold has also acknowledged that the mise-en-scène in *Phoenix*'s clinic is openly imitative of *The Face Behind the Mask*.[43]

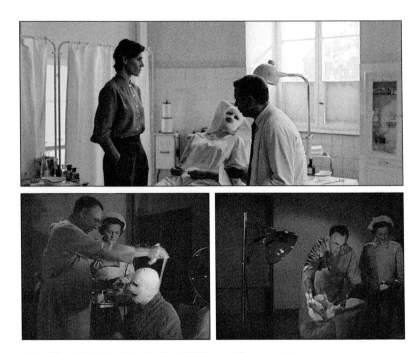

Robert Florey's *The Face Behind the Mask* (1941) as an influence on *Phoenix*.

As Nelly is being prepared for surgery, the doctor begins to put her under, and he distracts her by asking her to count backwards from ten. As she counts down, Petzold transitions to a different setting: a damp, dewy landscape in low light. A woman we assume to be Nelly gradually reaches a structure we later discover is the boathouse in which she hid from the Gestapo prior to her arrest and deportation. These memories are layered: we see traces of her internment, on the one hand, as indicated by her striped prisoner's uniform, and, on the other, we see her hiding place, just outside of Berlin. As she enters the boathouse we hear a single chord above the non-diegetic string music—a discordant note that disturbs or interrupts the harmonic ones. Her unconscious is telling her that something is off-key about Johnny, whose broad back can be seen at the piano. Neither wholly memory nor fantasy, this vision is a tangle of Nelly's traumatic past and wishful future; she is all at once the woman who is Johnny's wife and longs to see him again and she is also a still uniformed Holocaust survivor. Her face is enshrouded in darkness, and one cannot conclusively determine that Nelly is the woman in the dream. Her physiognomy remains illegible; she has returned to Germany as someone unrecognizable, even to herself. She is, on the one hand, wearing the striped camp uniform, but she is also lured to this place by Johnny, her Phoenix. The music he plays, this single discordant note, can hardly be considered orphic, and the fact that he does not turn to face her has less to do with the story of Orpheus and Eurydice than it does with her reluctance to be seen, even in a dream. Her facelessness represents an inward acquiescence to her loss of identity and to her overwhelming sense of shame.

Instead of a historical re-creation, Petzold offers a hybrid of fantasy and memory, one that, in the timing of its inclusion, calls to mind Vincent Parry's fantastical descent into unconsciousness as he is about to receive plastic surgery in Delmer Daves's *Dark Passage* (1947). Petzold's decision to include an associative dream at this point rather than a straightforward flashback is a choice against the direct representation or re-enactment of Holocaust atrocities. In this vision, Nelly is dressed as a prisoner, but she is by no means clearly positioned at or around Auschwitz. Petzold sketches out a fantasy that is based on but far from identical with her experience rather than staging a scene that re-creates the world of the death camps. In connection with the production of *Phoenix*, Petzold has spoken out about the inappropriateness of staging depictions of Holocaust atrocities, saying that depicting Auschwitz in a film suggests that it is something that can be repeated, which relativizes it. He says, "I would never film Auschwitz," adding that doing so would be "an impertinence" (*eine Unverschämtheit*).[44] His position resonates with older debates: when Jean-Luc Godard, for example, declined to

Nelly's traumatic memory combines uncomfortably with fantasy.

accept an award from the New York Film Critics' Circle in 1995, he explained that in rejecting the prize he was punishing himself for his failure "to prevent Mr. Spielberg from reconstructing Auschwitz" when he made *Schindler's List* (1993).[45] Some see rebuilding concentration camps, or shooting films at former camps, as tasteless, and, for some critics, it is especially disquieting when Germans do it.[46] Playing dress-up as Nazis and Jews is, from this perspective, a vulgarity. It is safe to assume that neither Godard nor Petzold would have attempted to make a film such as *Son of Saul* (2015), which claimed to depict with some degree of authenticity what death camps were like, and which won accolades for its purported verisimilitude.

It turns out that Petzold staged a Nazi death march for the sake of his film early in the production of *Phoenix* and that he then scrapped most of the footage, setting aside only a fragment of it to be used as part of Nelly's dream. In interviews, he has discussed how he filmed and then discarded the sequence, which was meant to have taken place just prior to Nelly's homecoming. It portrayed the fateful moments in which Nelly was shot and disfigured—the forced march in which she received her wounds as well as how she later regained consciousness among the other victims' bodies.[47] Petzold describes the footage as having been in poor taste, referring to its creation as "an infection of bad morality."[48] It is not the first time he worked this way: an opening scene of *Yella* (2007), staged as a callback to Hitchcock's *Marnie* (1964), was similarly filmed and scrapped.[49] However, his rejection of this type of historical recreation echoes Godard's criticism of *Schindler's List*, and the destruction of footage is a remarkably performative gesture. Was Petzold unaware of how he was going to feel about the sequence once it was complete? Did he undertake the project knowing that he might eventually declare it obscene and get rid of it? Claude Lanzmann, the late director of the epic Holocaust documentary *Shoah* (1985), believed that images of Holocaust atrocities—specifically, footage of Nazi violence as it is being committed—can never be comprehended insofar as no viewer who did not witness the horror first hand would be capable of fathoming its scope. Moreover, Lanzmann felt that such footage risked reproducing the dehumanizing gaze of the perpetrators who filmed it. He said that if he were to come into possession of footage of people dying in the gas chambers, he would destroy it.[50] Lanzmann's comments concerning the comprehensibility of the suffering in the camps applies to feature films as well, and he expressed, many times over, his objections to *Schindler's List*.[51] Such films tend to make the prisoners' suffering graspable, and their staged scenes of atrocities often come dangerously close to reproducing the standpoints of those responsible. Petzold's comments and his actions inscribe him into Lanzmann's discourse insofar as he, after re-creating and filming images of Holocaust violence, destroyed them out of concerns that they were obscene.

After her surgery, and while still in a dreamlike state, Nelly is roused by the intrusion of a doppelgänger: another patient, whose face is also wrapped in bandages, enters her room, standing briefly at the door. Their forms resemble one another, but based on the sequence of shots we are pointed toward the conclusion that the woman in the bed rather than the one at the door is Nelly. The double, in a shapeless gown, appears as an uncanny twin whose presence is meant to remind us of Nelly's fractured persona. This similarly defaced figure leads her down the clinic's corridor, and the sequence recalls Nina Hoss's movement through anonymous hotel hallways in *Yella*, scenes in which her character moves, as though she has been summoned, from room to room.[52] Entirely in white and treading slowly, the bandaged women in this sequence resemble ghosts, and the atmosphere of the encounter extends the dreamlike tone that was introduced during Nelly's surgical reverie. The enrobed woman—the one who appears to be Nelly—eventually arrives at her surgeon's workstation where she sees photographs of herself from the past. The doctor is working on the basis of a small archive of reference materials, spread out across a board. She surveys the drawings and

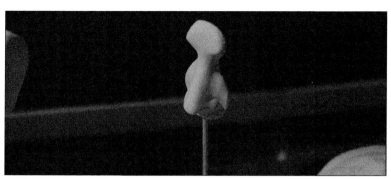

Nelly sees a sculpted model of a disembodied nose.

sketches, while her double takes a seat, squatting silently at her feet. Nelly first notices a sculpted model of a disembodied nose, and at the base of the model is her name. The nose, which is perhaps there to evoke the conversation Elizabeth Wolf had with her doctor about her Jewish features, can hardly be described as Jewish; it is just a nose. It is a part, rather than a whole, an approximate replica of a fragment of Nelly's physiognomy. The orphaned organ reminds Nelly that she may never be whole again. As she cannot see her own face in the space of a dream, she likewise cannot envision ever again being complete. At this moment there is no "she," just pieces of a self, severed from their origins. It is thus little wonder that her name, at the top of the board, is written in erasable chalk.

Because *Phoenix* is a film without flashbacks, one that contains none of the stylized journeys into memory typical of many Holocaust films, we are never provided with a clear picture of how Nelly looked prior to 1945. In accord with the logic of the film, in which Johnny willfully chooses not to see Nelly as she appears and to overlook the most obvious indications that she is who she is, we can assume that her physical transformation has not been radical; Johnny's inability to see her is more about his blindness than about any change in her appearance. The photo evidence confirms this; these photos of

Nelly looks at a snapshot of her and Johnny.

prewar Nelly are, as one would expect, also photos of Hoss, and they thus look similar to the woman we see throughout the remainder of the film, after the removal of her bandages.

Owing to a sign system consisting of crosses and circles, we are made aware that two of the women in the first photo became Nazi party members, and another died at some point more recently. Nelly is seen seated between the two remaining women, her arms around their shoulders. On one side of her is Lene and on the other is her cherished friend Esther, whose name Nelly adopts in the film's second half. The portrait of the six women is an exemplary illustration of German and Jewish camaraderie. Nelly then notices a second photo, in which her face is obscured by locks of hair. The picture has been folded back, and the part of the image that includes Johnny has been damaged, either deliberately by Lene or unintentionally by the surgeon. Nelly unfolds the photo, and her thumbs caress the snapshot's surface in an attempt to bring herself into physical contact with Johnny and with the past. It reminds her that she was once physically there, next to Johnny, while also serving as an emblem of a lost time. No matter how frequently and longingly Nelly's thumbs sweep over the image's surface, she cannot enter into the photograph; it is no time machine, and what is done cannot be undone.

A high-pitched note played by a stringed instrument creates a sound bridge to the following shot. Its whine may bespeak Nelly's anguish, perhaps because she still, at this point, has been mostly silent, but it may also stand in for Esther's voice insofar as Lene is on the verge of finding out that Esther was among the murdered at Auschwitz. The film cuts from the picture of Nelly and Johnny in Nelly's hands to an atrocity image: a photo of Holocaust victims. The photograph is out of focus, and only what we see through Lene's magnifying glass is sharp enough to discern. Petzold is obviously disinclined to provide a clearer image of Holocaust violence. The issue has arisen elsewhere in his work: in *The State I Am In* (*Die innere Sicherheit*, 2000), his teenage protagonist's class watches Resnais's *Night and Fog* at school, and Petzold integrates into his own film a brief clip from that famous and sometimes quite graphic documentary. Resnais's film includes images of Holocaust atrocities but Petzold decided not to include any of that film's explicit scenes. He shows instead *Night and Fog*'s contemporary color footage of camp ruins, images shot in the 1950s, after the camps had been abandoned. The footage used in *The State I Am In* begins with a shot of a chair in which prisoners may have been tortured, but tortured bodies are nowhere to be seen. Viewers who know *Night and Fog* will be aware of what is not shown. The Holocaust victims in the photograph in *Phoenix* also remain unseen; they appear only fleetingly and out of focus. These bodies, inasmuch as we can make any determination about them, intermingle with one another and, despite their enlargement in Lene's magnifying glass, might even be mistaken for tree limbs in a forest in winter.

Aside from the director's concerns about the obscenity of depicting atrocities, there may be a more pressing reason for leaving the photograph's minutiae out of focus: the technique of detection in which Lene is engaged stretches the limits of credibility, even for a fictional narrative film. It would be unusual for images to provide detailed information such as this in more than a small number of

A blurry photo of Holocaust victims, seen in Lene's magnifying glass.

cases. An image's resolution would have to be excellent to read ink markings that were once tattooed on emaciated bodies' arms, especially if the photographs were not taken for that purpose. Still more unlikely is that Lene would have found among the corpses the particular victim she sought. In this fictional sequence, however, she compares the information in front of her with the partially destroyed records from Auschwitz-Birkenau and determines that the number in question belonged to Esther, who apparently arrived at the camp in March 1943. It seems that Esther was not murdered upon arrival, but how she survived long enough so that she was not cremated prior to the camp's liberation, and how her tattooed limb happened to be among those photographed by the liberators are details that Petzold and Farocki's screenplay chooses not to pursue.

The two shots are linked in their depiction of the different techniques by which these photos are scrutinized. Petzold cuts from Nelly's gently caressing hands to Lene's analytic magnifying glass. One of the two photos Nelly examined was a photo of Esther, cheerful and alive, while Lene, at her desk, looks at this same woman, now as a corpse. For Lene, two layers of glass mediate between her and this image of death: the magnifying glass and her eyeglasses. Although both instruments help her see, they also shield her physically. Her apparently analytical disposition distinguishes her from Nelly, who runs her thumb across the photo in her hands, wishing she could penetrate it. For Lene, the past is an object of detection; she works on the basis of evidence and clues. For Nelly, by contrast, the past, the pre-war era, is a memory of a harmonious time. Nelly would like to fall into these photographs, but Lene can only steel herself against the shudder that will inevitably come from gazing at them for too long.[53] Lene's affect is unsustainable; she is on a road that eventually leads to her suicide. Atrocity images have their own gravity, and they eventually draw even the least morbidly inclined viewers into dangerously close orbit. What happened at the camps was too massive to comprehend, and Petzold and Farocki's premise is that the summer of 1945 was simply too soon after the war for survivors, whether they were returning from camps in Poland, from hiding in Switzerland, or from elsewhere, to process the catastrophe.

Night and Day

Phoenix waits some time before it finally reveals Nelly's unbandaged face. The film's second act opens three months after her return, as she, perhaps for the first time since the war, travels to Berlin's urban center. Lene brings Nelly to the site of the apartment she once shared

Nelly glimpses herself in the shards of a broken mirror.

with Johnny, and Nelly, like so many residents of Berlin at that time, wanders among ruins. Just beyond the entryway to what was her building, Nelly catches a glimpse of herself, reflected in shards of a broken mirror. Here we see two Nellys, one of whom is half faceless, a memory of a self she no longer resembles. In her current state, her identity has been fractured, and she sees herself in neither of these two reflections. Her image, had it been reflected in one piece, would have indicated that things could be made complete again—that what has been smashed was on the verge of being made whole. What Nelly sees, however, only highlights the extent to which her life has been shattered. The distress she feels as she encounters her own face, fragmentary and divided, propels her in the other direction, farther down the road, deeper down the rabbit hole of an idealized past.

More significant, however, may be the degree to which this scene will be familiar to viewers acquainted with German film. Nina Hoss's Nelly, catching sight of herself in a broken mirror, is standing in a position akin to that of Susanne Wallner, the heroine of Wolfgang Staudte's *The Murderers Are Among Us*, a film that was produced in Germany's occupied Eastern Zone in 1946.[54] Wallner is East German cinema's best-known returnee, its most famous *Heimkehrerin*. In that film, she has come back to her Berlin apartment in the hopes of leading a life similar to the one she had before: she wants to rebuild, and she eventually embarks on a romantic relationship with a man, a veteran suffering from post-traumatic stress, who ultimately becomes her partner in progress. Wallner is not a Jewish character, but one who had instead been deported from Germany as a political prisoner. That postwar film was aiming to reach a wide audience and, unlike *Marriage in the Shadows* (*Ehe im Schatten*, 1947), an East German film made in the following year that was based on the tragic fate of an interfaith couple, the actor Joachim Gottschalk and his Jewish wife Meta Wolff, during the Nazi era, *The Murderers Are Among Us* was not concerned with treating the Holocaust as a specifically Jewish or even a German-Jewish tragedy. It is thus deliberately imprecise about Wallner's backstory. Hildegard Knef plays the lead role, which transformed her into an iconic "rubble woman," a face of Germany's process of rebuilding. Petzold's near-replication of a shot from Staudte's 1946 film is by no means purely ornamental. He goes inside *The Murderers Are Among Us* in order to revise it. Resituating dimensions of Staudte's film, he replaces its German victim with a German-Jewish one. Nelly's homecoming is unique because she is a German Jew, and, in this way, Petzold and Hoss are rewriting Knef's iconicity.

Hildegard Knef's character became an icon, as did Hannah Schygulla's Maria Braun, and Nina Hoss's performance is meant to take its place alongside those. Like Maria Braun, Nelly is a woman who stands in for the fate of others at a particularly fraught historical moment. *Phoenix*'s inside joke about Maria Braun at its beginning (the moment when Lene says, "she's not Eva Braun"), would have accomplished something similar had it instead referred us to Knef's performance—the two characters, although differently styled "rubble women," confronted closely related challenges and hardships. Hoss has been cast in marquee roles along these lines before. Viewers of historical films might have already been familiar with her from *A Girl Called Rosemary* (*Das Mädchen Rosemarie*, 1996), one of her

Susanne Wallner (Hildegard Knef) returns to Berlin in *The Murderers Are Among Us* (1946).

first roles, in which she plays Rosemarie Nitribitt, a woman who manipulates men of means in order to make a living at the time of Germany's economic miracle, or from Max Färberböck's *A Woman in Berlin* (*Anonyma—Eine Frau in Berlin*, 2008) in which she plays a German journalist who was repeatedly raped by occupying Russian soldiers in the spring and summer of 1945, a woman whose fate came to be widely discussed in the German public sphere owing to her published memoir. The real-life protagonist of Färberböck's film had published her diary anonymously in order to avoid exposure and scandal, but because she chose to go unnamed, her story spoke to the experiences of the tens of thousands of women who had abided similar horrors in the period immediately after Germany's defeat. To look at *A Woman in Berlin* alongside *Phoenix* is to see Hoss portraying a German victim of Russian violence during the spring and early summer of 1945, and a German-Jewish victim of German violence in that very same summer and fall. One can easily imagine these two cinematic figures inhabiting neighboring areas of Berlin; the women's paths could well have crossed.

Looking at these two performances alongside one another, as two sides of a coin, one might think of two of the most well-known figures from German-language poetry, the two women in the Jewish writer and concentration camp survivor Paul Celan's "Death Fugue" ("Todesfuge"). That poem thematizes the fates of Margarete and Sulamith: Margarete is archetypically Germanic and bears the name of the blond-haired lover of Goethe's Faust, while Sulamith appears in the poem as her dark haired counterpart, a Jewish woman still covered in ashes from Nazi smokestacks. "Death Fugue," a poetic reckoning with the camps, was first drafted in 1945, in the same moment these two films are set, and Hoss, in playing these parts—in dramatizing the lives of these two victimized women—is both Färberböck's golden haired Margarete, oppressed and abused as a result of Germany's downfall, and Petzold's ashen-haired Sulamith, a newly liberated camp survivor. It is not entirely fair to identify the protagonist of *A Woman in Berlin* with Celan's Margarete; the diarist on whose story Färberböck's film is based had indeed supported the German war effort, but her story is much more focused on her victimization at the hands of Russian soldiers. The anonymous diarist and Nelly are, however, closely linked insofar as they are two portraits of women who suffered in the wake of the war, inhabiting the landscape of a destroyed city they once called home. They are also connected through their interrelated embodiments by Hoss. Understood in light of the two figures in Celan's poem, Petzold's film can be viewed as an address to Färberböck's, which appeared six years earlier. Despite the two directors' profoundly different styles, a few of the shot compositions in the one film seem to trade directly on the other, as though the locations of the two films—two soundstage empires of postwar rubble—had been purposefully interwoven.

But *Phoenix*'s main character might also have been influenced by two prominent Jewish "Nellys," each one helping to underscore how the film is a return to interrupted Jewish narratives, and an attempt to pick up where those histories were broken off: Nelly Sachs, for one, was a Berlin-born German-Jewish poet and playwright who barely escaped from Germany during the Second World War, having fled to Sweden in 1940. Sachs, who published the poem "Chorus of the Rescued" ("Chor der Geretteten") in 1947, which contains the lines, "our bodies continue to lament," and "the nooses wound for our necks still dangle," had an enduring friendship with Celan and is generally treated as one of the great German-language poets of the twentieth century.[55] Many Germans have tried to cast her as a figure of German and Jewish reconciliation particularly because she, similar to Petzold's Nelly, once had a romantic involvement with a non-Jew, and because her early poetry was strongly influenced by biblical imagery. Sachs, however, resisted conciliation with Germans after the war and opted to remain in Sweden. Despite the approbation and the prizes issuing from Germany, the Holocaust left her permanently estranged from her homeland. By virtue of being a Jewish Nelly in the postwar era, Petzold's protagonist brings some of this history with her into the film—the history of a Jewish exile who was, after the war, reluctant to renounce her resentment.[56]

When seen in light of the history of postwar German cinema, another Nelly comes to mind: the Nelly of Harald Braun's 1947 film *Between Yesterday and Tomorrow* (*Zwischen Gestern und Morgen*), which was produced in Germany's occupied Western Zone. Braun's film was shot in Munich and was among the very first German feature-length films produced in the postwar West. At the center of that film is the story of a Jewish woman from Munich, who in March 1938 returns to a hotel she had once frequented, knowing that she may be making herself vulnerable to her pursuers. That character's name is Nelly Dreyfuss, a somewhat over-determined name in this context insofar as one is likely to think of the Dreyfus Affair; she is, in other words, a representative Jew. Sybille Schmitz, who died tragically of an overdose in 1955 and who was the inspiration for Fassbinder's 1982 film *Veronika Voss* (*Die Sehnsucht der Veronika Voss*), plays Dreyfuss. As a non-Jewish German playing an earlier Jewish "Nelly," Schmitz is another intertextual figure for *Phoenix*. Her character's story is focalized through non-Jewish Germans; once again Hildegard Knef plays a practical and capable rubble woman, and the actor Viktor de Kowa, who participated in the production of several Nazi propaganda films during the Hitler years, plays the artist Michael Rott.

Between Yesterday and Tomorrow recounts Nelly Dreyfuss's story through flashbacks: like Nelly Lenz, the character is married to an ethnic German who divorces her under pressure. When the Gestapo comes to take Dreyfuss away, she commits suicide, hurling herself down the hotel's stairwell. Shortly before her death, she attempts to hide a valuable necklace—one that becomes a metonym for her absent body—and the film's main tension comes less from her experience of persecution than from Michael's vexation over the accusation that he had kept and sold the heirloom. His reputation is, in the end, restored; it is clear from the onset that he is of superior moral character and never would have done such a thing. Schmitz's Nelly dies, but we are supposed to feel that the Germans who survive carry her memory onward. The film contains no scenes of deportation, nor is there a Jewish survivor's homecoming; Dreyfuss does not return and therefore no longer haunts the city as an untidy remainder. Postwar German ethics are thus reconstituted over the body of a Jewish victim.[57] Her suffering was none of the protagonists' doing, and for this reason *Between Yesterday and Tomorrow* is a more agreeable, less inflammatory type of postwar film. Here, as in the case of Petzold's citation of The *Murderers Are Among Us*, elements of German cinema history are isolated and resituated so that pasted-over wounds can be opened.

A faint cross appears in one of Nelly's photographs.

After encountering her own distorted image and concluding that she can neither recognize herself nor be made whole again, Nelly steps back into the car with Lene and bemoans her fate: "There is no me anymore." She then asks Lene, "Would *you* recognize me?" Lene gives an affirmative answer: of course she would. Her devotion to Nelly is unmistakable, but Nelly remains incredulous. She then shows Lene one of the photos she has been holding onto since her time at the clinic. Strangely, this photo, one that we have seen before, now includes a faint cross over Nelly's head. Its appearance highlights this moment as a turning point insofar as it suggests that the old Nelly is dead. However, it raises questions: is the cross visible to the characters as well as the audience? Did Nelly put it there herself as an act of self-effacement?

As Hercules retrieved Alcestis from Hades in Euripides's eponymous play, Lene has retrieved Nelly back from the underworld, and like Charon, she has ferried her across the river, transporting her from hell into the light. All of this leaves Nelly indebted, which is ironic because she stands to inherit a substantial amount of family money that somehow escaped Nazi expropriation. In the moment she becomes moneyed, she finds herself beholden to others: she is not only indebted to Lene, but she also, because of her survival, owes a debt to her family members and to Esther. The German word for debt is *Schuld*, which also means "guilt" and is the root of the word "survivor guilt" (*Überlebensschuld*); the two concepts, guilt and debt, are closely linked. It is thus not only an unspoken air of erotic desire that hangs like a shadow over Lene and Nelly's relationship, but a sense of obligation as well.[58] Lene expects that the two of them will travel together to Palestine; she wants them to find a place in Haifa or Tel Aviv. It emerges fairly quickly that she has already been hunting for apartments on their behalf.

In the moment Nelly embraces Lene, in gratitude for all she has done, we hear a scratchy photograph recording of Kurt Weill singing "Speak Low," and even if this 1940s recording is perfectly appropriate to the period in which the film takes place, the record's scratchiness reads, to our contemporary ears, as an index of Nelly's nostalgia. Nelly wants to wipe the slate clean, to erase the recent past, because turning back the clock would expunge the balance sheet. Weill's song features prominently in *Phoenix*, appearing on the soundtrack in instrumental and traditional arrangements, and Nina Hoss sings it in the film's haunting denouement. Kurt Weill composed "Speak Low," and the American poet Ogden Nash is credited with having written its lyrics, although it is often said that Weill was the one who suggested the title. The song was first performed in the Broadway musical *One Touch of Venus* (1943), which is about the Ovidian metamorphosis of a statue, a fictional "Anatolian Venus" that comes to life. The song, "Speak Low," as sung by Venus, reminds its listeners that the time for love is always short, that the hour for it is eternally late, and that it invariably passes too soon.

When it was adapted into a film in 1948, the themes of *One Touch of Venus* were changed for more popular consumption. Instead of centering on a society that is so materialistic that it has forgotten about love, its producers emphasized musical comedy. Venus ends up inspiring the population to speak of love with one another, which results in a sudden upsurge in marriage licenses. Weill, another Jewish émigré like Lorre and Siodmak, fled Nazi Germany in 1933, and according to his biographer Foster Hirsch, he may have seen in "the misadventures of Venus on earth" an "allegory of his own experience as an 'alien' in America."[59] Hirsch asks, "Was [Venus's] odyssey somehow a submerged autobiography, a reflection of the way he and perhaps [Lotte] Lenya too had felt on their arrival in America in 1935 and perhaps still felt eight years later?"[60] Listening to Weill's vocal performance, Nelly and Lene are likely aware that they are listening to music made by a Jewish man who was forced out of Germany, and that this song was written after his arrival in the United States. As they discuss whether they will ever again be able to enjoy German music, the strains of "Speak Low" waft through the air as the work of an émigré, written in exile.

Lene has clearly longed to be with Nelly, to sit with her at dinner enjoying music, and as the two listen to "Speak Low," she asks, "Would you sing it for me?" Eventually, her wish will be fulfilled; Nelly's performance of the song at the film's climax is indisputably *for* Lene, but it only comes after her death. Nelly performs it for Lene in the sense that she is inspired by her memory, wielding the music as a weapon with which to wound Johnny. Lene's desires seem to center on their relationship, and although this dinner is intimate, the language of debt finds its way into the discussion: Lene declares that the two of them together will soon go and address Nelly's finances. The money, Lene explains to Nelly using plural pronouns and without a hint of uncertainty, belonged to those who were murdered, and it obligates *us* (*es verpflichtet uns*) to go to Palestine and found a state where "*we* Jews" can live safely and "take back everything *they* took from *us*." Lene overburdens this moment of intimacy with her resolute Zionism, and her language of *us* and *them* is awkward for Nelly. Setting aside the fact that Nelly still has Johnny very much on her mind, she also does not see herself as Jewish. She saw herself as more German than Jewish before the war, and unlike Elizabeth Wolf, who feels bound to the community of Jews through their common experience of persecution and suffering, Nelly prefers to place her hopes for the future in Johnny.

Veils worn by Nelly and by Maria Braun in Fassbinder's film.

The scene closes as we hear Weill's voice singing, "the curtain descends, everything ends," lyrics that at this point refer mostly to Lene's diminishing hopes for a shared future with Nelly. On the line "everything ends," Petzold cuts abruptly away, indicating a sharp disruption. Nelly's attentions are now elsewhere: in silence and with her eyes trained on the mirror, she prepares to go in search of Johnny. She dons a black veil, not because she is a mourner, but because she herself was thought to be dead. As an element of mise-en-scène, one can associate a veil like this with Maria Braun, who is wearing a veil when we first see her at the beginning of Fassbinder's film, being wedded to her beau Hermann, who is wearing his Wehrmacht uniform. Although the veil was not an uncommon accessory at the time, several scenes in which Maria Braun wears that veil are associated with her wartime marriage and with her attempts to keep that marriage alive. Nelly wants more to be Johnny's German wife than a Holocaust survivor living in Haifa, so she is likewise looking to revive her marriage, to make things "exactly as before." When she puts on the veil she looks like a bruised and battered Maria Braun, one with black eyes and a bandaged nose.

Long shadows populate Berlin's streets at night, which makes Nelly's journey to find Johnny resemble an excursion into land of the dead. She is living with one foot in the underworld, and the Berlin through which she walks is filled with shades. Shadows are a hallmark of German Expressionist film, but the audio, specifically

Shadows populate Berlin's streets at night.

the US soldiers' dialogue, brings Fassbinder to mind. It has a self-conscious artificiality to it, one that invokes the interactions between Maria Braun and that film's American troops. These are occupied streets, and in walking on them, Nelly is one of many German women under the occupation. She is, to some extent, playing the same role as Maria Braun—the German side of her German-Jewish self—and Petzold, at this moment, again invokes Fassbinder's film: he incorporates a blind street musician in dark glasses, one who makes us think of similar figures from Fassbinder's *The Marriage of Maria Braun* and *The Merchant of Four Seasons*.[61] The encounter with this busker is a stop on Nelly's journey through a shadowy postwar landscape, and when he directs her to the Phoenix nightclub, he plays the role of the blind Tiresias, who, during Odysseus's travels in the underworld, gave him important pieces of guidance.

In seeking out Johnny, Nelly makes her way to the Phoenix club. Outside the nightspot, she follows a man who is apparently also named Johnny, and who, in the darkness, she imagines might be *her* Johnny, down a shadowy passage. The idea that this man, who is seen shortly thereafter sexually assaulting a woman, could be her husband, suggests either that Nelly has always known that Johnny may be capable of such things, or that her experiences over the last year have bent her intuitive compass to the point of breaking. As a consequence of her uncertainty, Nelly stands on the spot too long, belatedly recognizing that she is in danger and attempting to flee. She excuses herself, saying, "I mistook you for someone," which is an ironic apology for her to be making in a film in which she is the subject of a major misrecognition, but when this alternate Johnny forcefully barks a militaristic "*Stehenbleiben!*," ordering her to "stand still," it provokes a traumatic fear response, immobilizing her. In word choice and tone, this is precisely what a camp commandant or a Gestapo agent would have called out, and her contact with this false Johnny foreshadows how the real Johnny will trade on her post-traumatic symptoms in order to manipulate her.

Upon Nelly's return from her expedition, Lene asks her whether she has given any more thought to whether she would prefer to live in Haifa or Tel Aviv. Sensing that Nelly needs encouragement, she mentions that she has found a Jewish choir in Palestine in which Nelly could sing. Nelly's exasperated response is: "What would I do in a Jewish choir?" She makes her point emphatically, declaring that she is not a Jew, and Lene informs her that she is one, whether she likes it or not. For Lene, the Holocaust should have served to remind Nelly that she has no choice in the matter; her heritage is not up for debate. Did she, while she was in Auschwitz, think only of her return to Johnny, never asking herself why she was being persecuted? Lene once again becomes a vessel for the transmission of a brutal truth: "They wanted to kill you because you are a Jew." In choosing to array their characters this way Petzold and Farocki alter the basic constellation of Monteilhet's novel. Elizabeth Wolf, returning from Dachau, had been well aware that she was Jewish, whether she wanted to be or not, and it was her husband Stanislas who, in one of the novel's flashbacks, expressed the idea that Judaism was neither a biological category nor Elizabeth's inexorable identity. Stanislas's position is self-interested and somewhat compromised insofar as he may be, it later emerges, concealing his own Jewish heritage, but from Elizabeth's standpoint his statements are simply naïve. This is the point at which she pushes back, informing him that "being a Jew means belonging to a community of suffering that the times have consolidated."[62] *Phoenix*'s screenplay here departs from Monteilhet: in the postwar era, the German denial of Jewish suffering effectively reconstructs Nelly, turning her into a Jewish survivor. She cannot remain on the German side of this historical divide. She is incontrovertibly a member of a community of suffering, persecuted at the hands of a "they"—as Lene says, "*they* wanted to kill you"—and, as if to make her point more forcefully, Lene chooses this moment to divulge further details about Johnny's betrayal: not only did *they* try to kill her because she was a Jew, but Johnny, the man in whom she has invested her hopes, may have helped them. As far as she is concerned, Nelly should not count on Germans to ameliorate her suffering, and Germany's continued hostility to its Jewish survivors may be the reason she provides Nelly with a gun, hoping, as she later admits, that Nelly will use it.

Why, under these circumstances, would Nelly, a German Jew, return to Germany at all? The plastic surgeon's question from the film's beginning remains unanswered. The sociologist Paul Massing, who was arrested in Germany in 1933 and eventually fled for Paris and the United States, co-authored an essay in 1945 entitled "Should Jews Return to Germany?" Massing theorizes that a Jew might return to "reassert the validity of his person" and demand the respect that was taken away.[63] He writes, however, that émigrés will never again encounter Germany as it was in the pre-Hitler days, and, according to Massing, they will never be taken for equals. German Jews, he concludes, are strongly advised to consider moving to Palestine.[64] His essay points toward "The Aftermath of Nazi Rule," Hannah Arendt's similarly themed essay from 1950 in which she writes about the lack of sympathy shown by many Germans, their refusal to face the horrors, and the apparent heartlessness they have shown Jewish survivors. Arendt outlines a typical scenario in which a Jew informs a German to whom he or she is speaking that they are, in fact, speaking with a Jew. After "a little embarrassed pause," she writes, the German will immediately switch the topic to German suffering, with the idea that one side cancels out the other.[65] The portrait she paints is by and large unforgiving.

As the history of every people, in Fritz Bauer's words, has its light and shadowy sides, Nelly's postwar life is separated into day and night: by day Lene tries to persuade Nelly to plan their transition to Palestine and think about their future. By night, however, Nelly tries to return to the past, hoping to reunite with Johnny. She waits patiently at the club, still veiled and dressed in black. Petzold describes the cabaret at the Phoenix as an attempt to recapture the spirit of an earlier time, the ambiance of Berlin in the 1920s and 30s.[66] The Phoenix club is a provisional effort to evoke the atmosphere of that city in its prime, and one of the stylized female singers on stage goes by the name Lola, an evocation of Marlene Dietrich's character in *The Blue Angel* (1930). The women's act features duets in which they alternately complement and mime one another's gestures. Their rendition of Cole Porter's "Night and Day" (1932) bespeaks several of the film's themes, in particular the two poles represented by Johnny and Lene. The wide-open eyes drawn on one of the vocalist's shoulder blades suggests that Nelly is continuously confronted by both yesterday's traumas and tomorrow's anxieties.

Echoing a similar scene in Thompson's film adaptation of *Return from the Ashes*, Nelly calls out to Johnny, who only glances vaguely in her direction. His eyes search the club, neither looking into the camera nor finding an eyeline match. In Thompson's film, the actress Ingrid Thulin's voice-over is, at that moment, steeped in despair: "Stan doesn't know me. He doesn't know who I am." At least one major German critic complained about the implausibility of this aspect of *Phoenix*'s premise. In a critical review for the highly regarded publication *Die Zeit*, Peter Kummel argues that the film thinks too little of its audience and gambles on its collective credulity:

A musical act at the Phoenix nightclub.

it would be unthinkable that a husband would not recognize his own wife, especially when confronted with her voice and bearing.[67] Those who criticize the film on this basis miss the point. Nelly may look the same, but *Phoenix* is about Johnny's blindness. The more she resembles herself, the more distasteful we find Johnny's inability to see what is right in front of him. The filmmakers' assumption may well have been that Nelly, after the war, looks in every respect identical to her past self, but that appearance is a construction of the beholder, and Johnny's failure to see is simply a refusal. In this film and in his next one *Transit*, Petzold simply asserts a significant or central narrative fact (about Nelly's changed appearance in the one case, and about the fascist occupation of France in the other) without making it part of the mise-en-scène. *Phoenix* is not asking its audience to be credulous, but is instead offering a conceit through which to understand the magnitude of Johnny's willful blindness.

This repudiation is a devastating experience for Nelly, who has so often envisioned their reunion. The cabaret performers' voices, now singing in English, flow into a harmony. They belt out Porter's playfully ambiguous lyric "Night and day / you are the *one*," the crowd roars approval, and Nelly bolts from the club, ashamed of her appearance and humiliated that she had allowed herself to hope.

She runs into the darkness and the rubble. It would seem that her trajectory is immediately followed by her return to the apartment—that she is running directly home—yet she re-enters the apartment in daylight. This feels very much like a continuity error, but the change had to occur: the apartment's sunlit spaces are the antithesis of the dark alleys outside the Phoenix club.[68] Johnny and Lene can, for Nelly, hardly coexist under any one sky; they are Nelly's night and day, two sides of a coin.

Johnny cannot see Nelly for who she is, so it stands to reason that he would only recognize her when she is mistaken for someone else. As herself, she is invisible to him, but that changes when a customer in the club assumes she is a prostitute. The "Night and Day" vocalists continue their routine on stage, shining spotlights into the audience in an imitation of Dietrich's performance in *The Blue Angel*. They sing the song "Berlin in Light" ("Berlin im Licht," 1928), which, like "Speak Low," is by Kurt Weill, but which was written before his emigration; pre-emigration Weill, associated with his time in Germany, thus plays at the club where Johnny works, while post-emigration Weill, associated with his move to America, plays in Lene's apartment. Nelly, however, does not hear the end of the song: as a result of the confusion about whether she is soliciting, she is escorted out—expelled again, in effect—without argument. Johnny pursues her, asking, as though he were talking to a stranger, whether she is looking for work. She only nods, voicelessly, in response to his questions. He leads her into dark alleyways, past the rubble and down some steps into a basement apartment in which a bare light bulb casts harsh shadows. There, he dictates his terms: Nelly will play the role of his wife, but she is not to use the familiar form of address with him. She is to stay in the apartment and not be seen outside. This is not the love nest she was hoping to share with him—it is a cell.

Nelly does not yet have both feet in the land of the living, so the space she now shares with Johnny must seem like a crypt, particularly in contrast with the brightly lit space in which Lene has housed her; the apartment she has been inhabiting, not to mention the cities of Haifa and Tel Aviv, depicted in postcard-style photographs, are sunlit places. But because Johnny is interring or entombing Nelly, effectively stowing her away and potentially re-traumatizing her, it might be seen as a reflex that she introduces herself to him with the name "Esther." This is not only a means of memorializing her murdered friend, but it is also meant to serve as a shield. In the fifth century BC, Esther, in disguise, informed the King about Haman's plot to kill the Jews. In so doing, she became a savior of the Jewish people. She is a symbol of defense and even retaliation, and her bravery is the basis of Purim. In taking the name, Nelly is incorporating Esther as well as fortifying a line of defense against Johnny. He expresses to her that there are not many people around named Esther, and the subtext is that there are not many Jews left in Berlin. Johnny, however, seems uninterested in further pursuing this line of thought. Its implications are remarkable; the idea that the woman he has decided to conceal in a dank cellar may be Jewish seems to have occurred to him, but he instantly sets this thought aside, preferring to concentrate on his moneymaking scheme.

Because Nelly is also beholden to Lene, who has surely noted her absence, she comes and goes from Johnny's basement. When she returns to Johnny a second time, he insists that she repeat her entrance. The exercise is confusing insofar as he hardly makes plain what he hopes to have her change. His didacticism is unproductive. He has her redo the arrival, once without her handbag, and he quickly becomes irritated with her. These lessons call George Cukor's *My Fair Lady* (1956) to mind, but in many respects they are more closely linked to scenes between James Stewart and Kim Novak in Hitchcock's *Vertigo*, which is among the most significant and recurring intertexts in *Phoenix*.[69] In this scene, Johnny coerces Nelly to perform a role that is entirely in his interest, just as Stewart's Scottie pressured Novak's Judy into remaking herself as Madeline.

Johnny is, however, an ineffective tutor: he barks instructions at Nelly until she eventually finds herself backed up against a bare wall, immobilized and uncertain about what to do. He then tries to send her away, pronouncing that the plan will never work and that she should take a couple of dollars and go, but she pleads with him, rushing to the table, her head sunken like a child's after having been disciplined, and she begs for another chance.

Seen from Nelly's perspective, each stage of this transformation is more degrading than the last. In the scene that follows, Johnny leaves her in the cellar with some food and a bit of homework: a handwriting exercise. After he returns from work, he calls her back to the table to practice writing. Forcing Nelly to rewrite her own words in this way is a harsh act of silencing; it transforms her into a copy machine. Either out of desire to please him or in the hopes that he will finally recognize her, she takes no pains to conceal that the original handwriting is hers, down to the signature. The woman seated before him must be none other than Nelly, but Johnny's self-interest and greed are ample enough that he remains blind to the uncanny similarity. He asks her to write the sentence, "I am alive and will soon return" (*Ich lebe und bin bald zurück*). Petzold and Farocki may mean for us to conclude that these words were lifted directly from correspondence Nelly sent after her deportation; some deportees—political prisoners, for the most part—were in fact made to write postcards to show that the concentration camps were not deadly. Such postcards would have been subject to censorship; they would have been compulsory lies, written under the gaze of watchmen. Now, Johnny is looming over Nelly, pressuring her into rewriting these words and thus re-experiencing a trauma.

Like the red light illuminating the outside of the Phoenix club, the redness of the dress that Johnny gives Nelly to wear hints at both eroticism and danger. It is decorated in lightly outlined images of falling leaves, ones that resemble pairs of red lips. If they are seen as sweet kisses, then they signal love, if they are seen as leaves, one

Petzold's composition is similar to Hitchcock's *Vertigo* (1958).

might instead be led to think of decay. But here Petzold may again have been thinking of *Vertigo*: not long after Scottie saves the woman he believes to be Madeline from drowning, she emerges from his bedroom wearing a similarly colored robe. Scottie had already imagined the two of them cohabitating like a married couple, and the dreamlike moment of her entrance, emerging from his bedroom in that silk robe, is the fulfillment of a wish.[70]

Although Nelly at one point awakens to a small breakfast and with the pleasant sensation that she might be living in the past, before any of this had happened, she quickly realizes that she is still in a nightmare. Johnny begins to badger her, first about dying her hair, and then with his plan to re-introduce her at the train station. Nelly protests that she would not return from a concentration camp looking so proper, but Johnny knows precisely what he intends. He tells her that no one wants anything to do with people who walk around with burned skin and shot-up faces; they want Nelly, he explains, not "a ragged camp internee." He seems to have a deep understanding of German indifference, including, most likely, his own. It is his intention, in any case, to use that indifference to his advantage.

As if overtaken by a sudden paroxysm of truth, Nelly recounts for Johnny a memory about the practices of the *Effektenlager* at the Auschwitz complex in which the stolen property and clothing of arriving deportees were inventoried. The recollection pours out of her, and we are meant to hear it as though it were being spoken for the first time. As Nelly reaches her story's climax, Johnny is already asking, "Where do you know this from?" It does not occur to him that these are events from Nelly's past, and that she is testifying to something she survived. She says only that she read it, answering with the single word "gelesen," which negates the authenticity of her testimony, framing it as someone else's story. That this simplistic explanation satisfies Johnny is proof that he would prefer not to hear about her past. The story she tells recalls that of Erika Rothschild, a German-speaking Auschwitz survivor who was born in Bratislava, and who testifies before the camera in Erwin Leiser's Holocaust documentary *We Were Ten Brothers—The Road to Auschwitz* (*Zehn Brüder sind wir gewesen—Der Weg nach Auschwitz*, 1995). In that film, Rothschild describes how she was forced to work in a women's commando, sorting the possessions of those who had been gassed. One day, she came across a handbag her father had given her mother, which was filled with her mother's possessions. She concludes her testimony with the claim that something broke inside of her that day, which was never again made whole.

A related account can also be found in the Austrian-born director Fred Zinnemann's narrative feature film *The Search* (1948), which was released in Germany in 1961. Near its very beginning that film depicts occupation authorities in Bavaria immediately after the war interviewing children, mostly former camp internees, who have been displaced. A young dark-haired girl from Budapest whose parents were gassed at Dachau explains that her task was to go through the clothes of prisoners who had been executed, to sort them according to size in a room adjacent to the crematorium. There, among the clothes, she says, she found her mother's blouse. *The Search* is only a feature film, and it is by no means a reliable source of Holocaust testimony, but Zinnemann's scene is extraordinary in its groundbreaking depiction of the process of recording survivors' accounts in the wake of the war, when it was still, for most, too soon to understand the scope of what had happened. Eyewitness testimony's value was, at that time, not generally recognized; its widespread collection came only later. As far as the story's appearance in *Phoenix* is concerned, the Hungarian girl's testimony may have been overheard, colportaged, one might say, from one film to the next. For his part, Zinnemann was a Jew who began his career in film together with Wilder and Siodmak, but came to America prior to the Nazi takeover. He was, like Lubitsch and Edgar G. Ulmer, an émigré who became a "de facto exile."[71]

The assurance that their German acquaintances will be uninterested in the past comes easily from Johnny. The idea that no one would want anything to do with a former camp internee was already clear to Arendt in 1943 when she explained why Germany's various refugees were disinclined to discuss their experiences in concentration camps. Arendt writes, "how often have we been told that nobody likes to listen to all that; hell is no longer a religious belief or a fantasy, but something as real as houses and stones and trees."[72] Arendt's point extended beyond just Germans. "Nobody," she writes, "wants to know that contemporary history has created a new type of human beings—the kind that are put into concentration

A young girl from Budapest tells her story in *The Search* (1948).

camps by their foes and internment camps by their friends."[73] The memory Petzold's Nelly recounts here is quite different from the story associated with Nelly Dreyfuss in *Between Yesterday and Tomorrow*, who throws herself down a stairwell off screen, falling out of sight, while the film's German protagonists dedicate themselves to preserving her memory, a memory in which concentration camps play no role. That film is closer to how most—not only Germans, but, according to Arendt, most of the world—preferred to have Holocaust stories told.

If Nelly, when she was married to Johnny and before she was an Auschwitz survivor, once aspired to resemble Hedy Lamarr, she now sets out to do so again. In an effort to sustain Johnny's charade, and to continue to be, at whatever cost, in proximity to him, she continues her bid to transform herself. The Austrian-born Lamarr, after ending her marriage to a domineering husband, abandoned her film career in Nazi Germany and fled, first to London and then, eventually, in 1938, to Hollywood. By 1945 Lamarr would have been known to Nelly as an icon of self-determination. As "Esther," Nelly is considering whether she can transform herself back into Nelly's one-time ego ideal. Following the exceedingly difficult conversation in which she, for what may be the first time, speaks aloud about her experience in the camps, the suggestion that she should now stylize herself as a movie starlet seems perverse. The gap between her experience and Johnny's role-playing game takes a persistent psychic toll.

Writing in 1980 for the German journal *Filmkritik*, Farocki composed an essay about the motif of "transposed" or "swapped" women (*vertauschte Frauen*) in film.[74] Farocki writes that the common way to tell the story of the transposed woman is by creating two characters who resemble one another, and then by having their transposition, or their exchange of roles, fail. Imperfect exchanges leave behind remainders. Farocki notes that it is more often women that are exchanged in film, although male war survivors and veterans have been exchanged with one another as well, as in the case of the Martin Guerre films. Farocki's point is that these sorts of masquerades, as a conceit, are a means of rendering changed perceptions material, and an obvious touchstone for his argument is *Vertigo*. He also refers readers to *The Phantom Lady*, a Cornell Woolrich story that Robert Siodmak turned into a film in 1944.[75] Like Siodmak's *The Dark Mirror*, that film is a reference point for *Phoenix*: Nina Hoss is stylized such that she resembles the star Ella Raines, and Johnny looks like the American actor Alan Curtis, down to the thin mustache. (The other influence on Johnny's appearance is that of the bedraggled Tom Neal in Edgar Ulmer's *Detour* [1945], a film the cast is said to have watched during the production of *Phoenix*.[76]) Farocki summarizes that in *The Phantom Lady*, the vanishing woman to whom the title refers has not been transposed with another woman, "but rather with nothingness."[77] Siodmak's film is paradigmatic where the misrecognitions in *Phoenix* are concerned: Nelly is trying to become an irrecoverable, pre-war version of herself—a past self that no longer exists and cannot be retrieved.

Johnny resembles Alan Curtis, star of Robert Siodmak's *The Phantom Lady* (1944).

In pursuing this phantom version of herself—in vainly trying to turn back the clock—Nelly is devoting herself to putting her relationship with Johnny back on track. She peers out the basement window, watching him return, and the perspective suggests that she has been waiting for him. He enters, and it is apparent that she has caught his eye, but Petzold doesn't cut to her immediately; once again, her appearance is revealed to us through the facial reactions of another. There is a currency in moments of uncertainty, as in the brief parts of *Vertigo* in which we as viewers do not yet know whether Judy and Madeline are really the same person. In Johnny's basement apartment, it seems for a moment that Johnny might be seeing Nelly *as* Nelly, that the charade will come to an end, and that the confusing remainder will be washed away. We hear Nelly pose the question "Do you recognize me?" in its entirety before Petzold cuts to a medium shot of her, and we see that she is presenting herself, as best she can, as a woman who resembles Hedy Lamarr. She approaches Johnny from the depths of the frame, moving toward the viewer as the camera gently eases toward her, and she is likely hoping that this is the final stage of her transformation: from crossing the bridge at the beginning, she has at last arrived, to be reunited with him and recognized as the person she once was. Stray shadows cast by locks

Similar scenes in *Phoenix* and Hitchcock's *Vertigo*.

of hair partially veil her face. Johnny is immobilized, and the scene's tension comes from an uncertainty as to whether the truth will be revealed. But Johnny's blindness is stubborn: Nelly approaches and he says, "that's enough"; as far as he is concerned, Nelly is not meant to arrive—she is still unwelcome in the world of the living.

The scene is recognizably related to the corresponding sequence in *Vertigo*, in which Judy, in almost identical fashion, approaches Scottie from the depths of the image, sauntering into the foreground dressed as Madeline. She walks toward Scottie with a hopeful expression on her face, one similar to Hoss's. But where the emphasis in that film fell on Scottie's euphoria, it now falls on Nelly's disappointment. In *Vertigo*, the two principals kiss, and Hitchcock concludes the scene with a romantic and exhilarating circular pan. Viewers would be apt to recognize Petzold's allusion; we expect, whether based on our acquaintanceship with *Vertigo* or as a reflexive response, that this scene will also end in a kiss. However, Johnny's insistent "that's enough" brings everything to an abrupt conclusion. His cooperation with her extends only as far as the particulars of his scam. His voice resembles that of a director calling for a cut. There will be neither a kiss, nor a 360-degree pan.

Holding at all costs to his plan, Johnny proceeds in accord with the premise that the two of them are strangers. The high wire they walk in ceaselessly repressing the past—Johnny's unwillingness to hear about the Holocaust and Nelly's inability to speak about it—leaves them both in a vertiginous state. Ever more eager to assert control, Johnny attempts to further detain Nelly. He proclaims that she is not to go outside at all, but she panics, and is, at this point, clearly reliving her confinement in the houseboat where she hid from the Gestapo before her deportation. She pleads and finally convinces Johnny to join her outside. He agrees, although he apparently stipulates that she has to conceal herself behind her hat and veil. She is still, despite the surgery and the passage of time, a woman denied the right to a face.

In Nelly's eagerness to restage the high points of their romantic life, she shepherds the two of them over to a familiar park bench. To Johnny, it looks as though she is striking a pose modeled on a photograph, and he accuses her of imitating one of the pictures from his collection. He sounds as though he is trying to convince himself rather than her when he growls: "Stop playing Nelly. I know that you are not Nelly. You don't have to convince me." He speaks as though he were simply entitled to treat her that cruelly. Moreover, the outburst is nonsensical, even paradoxical: why would Nelly be attempting to convince him that she is *not* Nelly? The case is quite the opposite; she would like to return them both to the past. As an accusation, it makes little sense, and Johnny's muddled thinking bespeaks his escalating vertigo; he is, despite his intentions, convincing himself of something after all.

As with Johnny's insistence that Nelly remain in the basement, his fervid resolve that she not be seen outside or sit on a public bench replays for her the time she spent in hiding and fearing denunciation. Yanking her from the bench for fear of being seen, Johnny might as well be telling her that the bench is reserved for Aryans, as some benches in Germany had been. In an interview, Petzold refers to how Germans and Jews were unable to return to how things were prior to the war, because everything, even an object as common as a chair, took on different meanings in the postwar years.[78] Johnny seems unaware of the side effects of his actions, specifically all that he is subjecting "Esther" to in the interest of greed. Here, near the end of *Phoenix*'s second act, we see the extent to which the film is focused on continuities from 1945 rather than new beginnings. While many films, such as *The Murderers Are Among Us* and *Between Yesterday and Tomorrow*, were aimed at turning the page, *Phoenix* asserts that the Zero Hour was a fabrication, and that there was no blank slate. New days, such as they are, are bound to carry with them the past's complications.

The Curtain Descends

Insofar as Nelly's life has been divided into night and day, into Lene's light and Johnny's shadows, then these spheres, at the beginning of the film's final act, eclipse one another. The last interaction between Lene and Nelly begins in near total darkness. Only a thin sliver of light, a small halo, can be seen reflecting from Nelly's silhouette, as she explains to Lene the significance of her longstanding hope for a reunion with Johnny. She explains all of this with more than a little disregard for how hurtful it must be for Lene. The role is familiar: in Thompson's film adaptation of *Return from the Ashes*, it was Dr. Bonard, patiently but gloomily waiting for the object of his desire to realize the truth, and in *Vertigo* this burden fell on Midge, Scottie's stalwart and apparently chaste supporter. Lene's glare is penetrating as she listens to Nelly report that she felt dead when Johnny first misrecognized her but that she now feels alive again. She speaks of her renewed life in the third person, recounting, "I'm really jealous of me." The line is taken from Monteilhet's novel, and *eifersüchtig*, the word for "jealous" that is used here, was also the one chosen by the novel's German translator.[79] Nelly neither recognizes Lene's desire to be with her, nor does she seem to recall that it was Lene who retrieved her, bringing her back to the world of the living. To see Nelly shrouded in darkness is to see her from Lene's perspective. When Nelly says that Johnny has made her feel like herself again, the statement comes as a devastating blow, and it is followed by another: "I cannot come to Palestine." As far as Lene, who, when she speaks of Nelly speaks of *we* and *us*, is concerned, Nelly is not only declining her own redemption, but also *their* freedom, and *their* future.

Lene is a figure we associate with Arendt, who stared Germans' culpability and lack of compassion directly in the face, yet she is also stylized after Jean Améry, an Austrian Jew who survived Nazi torture and committed suicide in 1978. He is one among a number of ghosts that Lene's character imports into the film. Having gone to get a cigarette and changed her placement such that she is elevated, no longer listening but now lecturing, Lene channels Améry, providing an astonishingly short but to the point history of twentieth-century German and Jewish relations. The Jews, she says, wrote, sang, slaved, and went to war for Germany, but still they were gassed "one and all." The word she uses for "slaved" is *malocht*, a Hebrew word for heavy work that entered into German via Yiddish; the word self-consciously identifies her speech as Jewish. And now, she concludes, the survivors return from the camps and forgive, which is something she cannot abide. Apart from the fragment of the suicide note we later hear in voice-over, this is Lene's final exchange with Nelly, and her discourse echoes Améry's 1966 essay "Resentment," in which he expresses his unwillingness to forgive Germans. As Hannah Arendt

Lene lectures Nelly.

before him, Amèry describes encounters with Germans who would prefer not to direct blame toward Germany, who feel they had no part in the past's tragedies, and who are uninterested in hearing his story.[80] He explains at length why he felt no obligation to help Germans move on and how he would prefer to compel the perpetrators to exist in the same traumatic moment at which his own personal history was brought to a standstill, specifically, his experience as a victim of torture. Lene echoes Amèry's acknowledgment of his desire for revenge, particularly when she says that it would have been preferable to her had Nelly shot Johnny.

If Lene has taken on the qualities of "night," insofar as she is an embodied acknowledgment of anger and resentment, Johnny now appears to inhabit Nelly's daylight. She boards the back of his bike, and the two set out on a midday ride. As signaled by the sound of a cathedral bell, their trip is counterpart to the daytime excursion to the Mission San Juan Bautista in *Vertigo*. Nelly would not be wrong to imagine this as a date, an opportunity for them to leave the city behind. The trees they pass in these north German woods may act for some as a callback to the woods in Petzold's *Barbara*, in which long bicycle rides were a major motif. These scenes in *Phoenix*, in carrying the memory of the earlier film with them, simultaneously

Nelly rides on the back of Johnny's bike.

trade on and repudiate the hope that these two will pick up where that film's storyline ended.[81]

Apart from the absence of her camp uniform, Nelly's return to the boathouse repeats many elements from the dream she had in the clinic. Once she is inside, she stares at what appears to be a blank wall until she opens a hidden door. Because the door did not appear in her earlier dream, we may conclude that it, along with the details of her concealment, have been repressed in memory. Behind the panel are a bed frame, a metal cup, and a small lamp; it is a cell within a cell, hardly a humane space for a person. Johnny comes thundering in, never having lived in fear of loud noises in this place as had Nelly. His question, "What are you doing here?" (*Was machen Sie hier?*) is the same one a Gestapo agent might have asked, and it awakens a traumatic response, driving Nelly to back up against the wall. Petzold used this shot composition before, when they were in Johnny's basement, and it is one we see later in the film, when they are in a hotel room together. Nelly's traumatic distress is akin to the vertigo experienced by James Stewart's Scottie when he climbs the missionary tower. In Nelly's case, it can be described as an attempt to make herself invisible, to pass through the solid wall and return to the safety of her hiding place.

Nelly attempts to make herself invisible.

As they ride back to the city on Johnny's bike, Nelly, still speaking as though she were not herself, asks him, "Did you betray Nelly?" She poses the question in a way that indicates her awareness that she might not receive an answer. Her voice is low, and she directs her comments into his broad shoulder, as though she were talking to herself.[82] Yes, she continues, perhaps Johnny led the police to her, but this was not a real betrayal—he simply went to check on her after he'd been interrogated, and he ended up being followed. He might have given her away, in other words, without knowing it. The story with which she provides him would be a credible alibi, were he to want one, but there is no evidence that any of this is of interest to him. He is more interested in making preparations for the next stage of their deceit. In elaborate detail, he tells Nelly precisely what will happen when they perform her return, and all of this dramaturgy is just short of a dress rehearsal. He tells her exactly what her former acquaintances Sigrid and Monika will say when they first see her, and how they will embrace her. He plays the part of a director, scripting and blocking a bittersweet scene of homecoming, one that offers the certainty of an exultant postwar reconciliation.

Because of the time Nelly has invested in rehearsing her role with Johnny, she has neglected her relationship with Lene. Upon her return to their sunny apartment, she wonders why everything is so soundless, apart from the telltale ticking of a clock. Nelly then notices the letter of reference for Frau Schwarz, who enters and informs her that there is a letter for her as well. Frau Schwarz reports that Lene shot herself. She then leaves Nelly alone, and the loose cinematic frame emphasizes Nelly's isolation. Despite the fact that she is at the frame's center, she seems small and ensnared. We do not know enough about Lene's decision apart from the fact that staring at images of the dead seems to have taken its toll on her, and that she has been saddened by her failure to convince Nelly to leave Germany behind. In *Vertigo*, as Chris Marker notes, the would-be paramour Midge was driven from the film two-thirds of the way through, a departure he describes as "probably unparalleled in the serial economy of Hollywood scripts."[83] Midge and Lene exit the film at similar points, meaning that these films' last acts take place entirely without them; Scottie and Nelly are each left without their supporters, faced with troubles of their own making. For her part, Lene's suicide inscribes her in a history of Holocaust and post-Holocaust era Jewish suicides, from Benjamin and Stefan Zweig to Levi and Améry, who killed themselves long after the war's end. If Lene feels closer to the dead than she does to the living—if she feels accountable to them—then this is one way of satisfying their demand. The suicide also represents an effort to get through to Nelly, to make sure that the message to her, such as it is, reaches its destination.

The film is, at this point, advancing toward a theatrical conclusion in which Nelly will play the lead role in Johnny's production. As they ride on Johnny's bike to the train station, Lene's voice can be heard speaking aloud the text of her suicide note. The fact that she speaks over these images and from the grave provides her with the authority to enframe the sequence. Her words and Johnny's actions cut against one another, her truths undermining his deceits. The letter ascribes a joint fate to her and Nelly: she explains, "There is no going back for us." She then, however, adds a corrective: "But for me there is also no going forward." Though Lene is a different kind of Holocaust survivor from Nelly—she is not "from the camps"—her suicide is surely explicable as a Holocaust aftereffect, and her note leaves Nelly with responsibilities. Lene's point of view corresponds to the sentence Monteilhet wrote for Elizabeth Wolf about belonging to a community of suffering; Lene speaks of "*our* dead" and "*our* living," and from her point of view, Nelly is, like her, a Jew, whose fate is, whether she likes it or not, consolidated with that of others.

The voice-over is not only Lene's final testament, but it also informs Nelly as to the truth about her marriage, a story that serves as a counterpoint to the often-mythologized narratives of German and Jewish loves that predated the war. Petzold and Farocki were likely drawn to Monteilhet's novel in part because of its lack of sentimentality about the Jewish and Gentile affair at its center. Stanislas married Elizabeth Wolf on a whim, more to prove a point than out of love, which puts the storyline on altogether different footing from that of German films such as *Gloomy Sunday* (*Ein Lied von Liebe und Tod*, 1999), *Aimee & Jaguar* (1999), and *Rosenstraße* (2003), each of which highlight positive, even redemptive portrayals of interfaith love. Those award-winning German narrative features depict German culture—minus a handful of brown-shirted bad-apple exceptions—as uniquely eager to engage in affectionate and productive symbiosis with German Jews. *Phoenix* does not reveal whether Johnny ever really loved Nelly, but Lene, after her death, gets to have the final word on the matter. The proof of what she considers to be Johnny's betrayal is revealed by her voice-over and is timed precisely to their arrival at the station, as daylight transitions to night. On this train platform, which eerily resembles a stage, Johnny will insist that Nelly take part in a crass spectacle, a callous reminder of what was assuredly a painful deportation.

If we can describe Johnny's behavior as cruel, his cruelty is predicated on the assumption that he knows, on some level, with whom he is dealing. Either the woman in his presence is a stranger named Esther, who may be Jewish—and what, if that is the case, did "Esther" endure during the war?—or he is in fact dealing with someone he knows, consciously or semi-consciously, to be his former wife, and he has no compunction about re-traumatizing her. Given that both of those assumptions are possible and that one of them is likely true, his suggestion that she permit him to create a scar on her arm for the sake of his production crosses what may be a final line.[84] After hiding her from the world, for the second time, in his basement, and after planning to have her re-enact parts of her deportation, he now wants to scratch into her skin, an activity that would reproduce the sadistic process of Nazi tattooing, while also erasing the historical evidence of her trauma. The procedure he proposes also has to be understood relative to her plastic surgery: Nelly arrived back in Germany with the intention of writing over her wounds, to have them erased, and erasing her tattoo might, in this sense, have been what she wanted all along. But she now begins to see the erasure of the wound as the erasure of her experience. For Primo Levi, his Auschwitz tattoo stood for the experience *in nuce*. He writes that the tattoo's symbolic meaning "was clear to everyone: this is an indelible mark, you will never leave here; this is the mark with which slaves are branded and cattle sent to the slaughter, and that is what you have become."[85] *Phoenix* is set in the immediate aftermath of the war, and the tattoo's significance is beginning to dawn on Nelly. Johnny is on the verge of assaulting her with a knife before she recognizes that erasing the mark would be a step towards erasing her past, and that it would compound the original act of violence.

Although Nelly first returned with the wish that she could become a pristine writing surface—that the new Nelly would disappear and the old one would return—she ultimately changes her mind. Turning back the clock would mean forgetting the real Esther and now Lene as well. Whether as an angel of history or a Jewish Phoenix, her burden is to recall the dead. Levi, who felt it was his obligation to convey, inasmuch as it was possible, what happened at Auschwitz, wrote: "At a distance of forty years, my tattoo has become a part of my body. [...] Often young people ask me why I don't have it erased, and this surprises me: Why should I? There are not many of us in the world to bear this witness."[86] Dora Apel sees a connection between the process of tattooing at Auschwitz and Nazi race politics insofar as the tattoo provided a mark of physical difference, where the racial differences were constructed and imaginary. Pointing to the Jews' overall identicalness with other Europeans, Apel writes, "For decades before the war, the dominant trend for most French and German Jews was to blend in with the majority culture. In an attempt to achieve even greater invisibility in the 1930s, more and more German Jews actually went uncircumcised, a remaining marker of difference."[87] Because Nazi racial thinking was essentially a fiction, Nazi ideology was, according to Apel, driven to impose another physical mark. Nelly, who seems to have believed her Judaism was invisible, and who had no reason not to see herself as German, now, owing to the tattoo, possesses a physical sign of difference. To possess it is to own her Judaism.

Johnny has already created a figurative scar by ignoring Nelly's past, and the literal act of violence against her sends her scrambling away. Taking a moment alone in the washroom, Nelly eyes the gun in her handbag. Like a wolf at the door, Johnny appears in a shadowy outline, and her decision *not* to shoot him is a decision against the conventions of film noir, which usually requires a murder.[88] Killing him would mean the excision of a protagonist whose behavior is continuous with the past, and sacrifices of that sort were often called for in postwar films, but any film that speaks critically to that tradition would also have to repudiate its straightforwardly cathartic conclusions. Petzold and Farocki have Nelly consider murder, but she instead sets the gun aside and pulls out the paperwork that Lene left her. Nelly looks at the letter, written on Reich stationary from October 1944, which confirms that she (and here her last name is revealed to be "Wolff") was divorced from Johnny with his consent. As she stares at this piece of evidence, we hear the echo of a train engine and its whistle. The subtext of the audio cue is unmistakable: Johnny's signature triggered her deportation.

Petzold cuts abruptly to a shot of Nelly amidst the crowd in a train car. The tight frame indicates that she is literally and figuratively penned in. The setting looks more or less ordinary—it is a typically crowded train car—but for her the scenario likely echoes her deportation. Susanne Wallner's return to Berlin by train at the beginning of *The Murderers Are Among Us* was meant as a reversal, and a homecoming can certainly be interpreted as an "anti-deportation"—as long as there is a home to return to. Nelly's world, however, is less like home to her with each passing day. When she arrives on the platform, Sigrid approaches her first, just as Johnny said she would. He had guaranteed that she would run up and say: "I can't believe it," and that their friend Monika would then approach Nelly and say something about her dead husband. This is precisely what happens, and the accuracy with which Johnny had described the scene suggests that he may have coordinated these acquaintances' reactions as well. If he had indeed planned with the circle of friends, step by step, their responses, then for whose benefit has this show been staged?

The ensuing scene is perverse and might have had its place in an otherworldly film by Luchino Visconti or David Lynch: Johnny has organized a garden party for his survivor wife, and members of the group make toasts, addressing their remarks to her. Their friend Alfred says that "we" missed you and talks about a bench on which she and Johnny used to sit. This is perhaps the same bench on which Johnny prevented her from sitting earlier. Alfred continues, adding the strange and revealing sentiment, "And now you're sitting here, Nelly. And I do not have to close my eyes to see you." They all drink to Nelly, who remains silent and in this way unseen. Her role at this reception is not to speak; her enforced silence is a means of preventing her from giving deliberate or inadvertent vent to her

Nelly amidst the crowd in a train car.

wrath, from becoming an angry Phoenix. What would Nelly say were she to open her mouth? In a toast to her, Johnny says that Nelly is his love and his life, "no matter what happened" (*egal was passierte*). His words are essentially a promise of forgiveness: the Holocaust is water under the bridge. The crowd seems to approve of this idea, specifically, that it is incumbent on the Germans to forgive the Jews for Auschwitz, for the disruption in German history, for their losses, for their embarrassment, and for the difficult conditions in which the German nation presently finds itself. The attitude is consistent with so-called secondary anti-Semitism, or the phenomenon of associating Jews with the sullying of German history, even blaming them for it, a phenomenon diagnosed at the end of the 1950s in the wake of a series of anti-Semitic attacks in Germany.[89] Johnny's preposterous sentiment is met with uniform agreement: the entire group applauds as though they have just witnessed a top-notch theatrical production.

Nelly suggests that they all move inside, and everyone follows her. Johnny had been acting as the director of a staged proceeding, but Nelly now adopts that role. The change signals an end to her helplessness. Control is being wrenched away from Johnny, a turn that began at the moment Lene's voice-over was introduced. Nelly instructs him to play "Speak Low," and he looks surprised. If Johnny believes that the woman in front of him is not actually Nelly, then the risk to him is high: her singing, as dispositive as a fingerprint, would make it clear to his carefully chosen witnesses that she is the false Nelly. He warily begins, and Nelly lets the first cue pass her by. When she eventually begins to sing, apprehensively and off key, the group may suspect that something is wrong. She then, however, changes her tune: no longer beholden to Johnny and this forced theatrical production, she hits the right notes.

"Speak Low" is written for piano and voice, and they are all that one hears in Weill's version, which played earlier in Lene's apartment. Most interpretations of the song such as Billie Holiday's 1956 rendition rely on the vocalist taking latitude and unfastening him or herself from the piano's rhythmical constraints. The song is about love, yet the instrument and voice may dramatically diverge, and the composition calls, at its end, for a nearly spoken vocal part, a quasi-parlando that highlights the singer's emancipation.[90] But Nelly breaks off before that; even the song's famously irresolute ending would bring too much closure to this scene. After she sings the line, "tomorrow is near / tomorrow is here / and always too soon," Johnny is immobilized; he stops playing and finally understands. The revelation has unfolded gradually and painstakingly over the course of the song, and at the end of the word "soon," Petzold cuts to Nelly's arm, her sleeve rolled up, displaying the tattoo, which speaks even more loudly than her singing voice. Johnny recognizes what we as viewers have known all along; she was in Auschwitz and she bears its mark like a Homeric scar. The plastic surgery at the film's beginning is now set against the brazen display of her tattoo at the end; the two moments constitute the story's frame. Whereas Odysseus's scar was proof of his identity, Nelly's tattoo establishes that she has become a different self—she has, in fact, journeyed away from home and returned with the identity of a Jewish Holocaust survivor. The tableau of Germans looking on resembles the photograph we were shown of this same group earlier in the film. Their silent stare is perhaps

Johnny and his friends have difficulty assimilating new information about Nelly.

meant as a reflection of the film's German audience; Nelly's vocal performance is a function of her testimony, and the information is, for them, difficult if not impossible to absorb.

Despite what Johnny perceives during this denouement, he now resembles a man who sees and hears nothing more than the magnitude of his appalling error. He appears to be staring into empty air, and his expression resembles the look on Scottie's face at the very end of *Vertigo*, when he realizes that his stubbornness has left him with nothing and no one, a look of astonishment that asks, "What have I done?"[91] In silence, Nelly reaches with her tattooed arm for her jacket, across the entirety of the frame. The focal length then adjusts such that the space into which she begins moving, through the length of the room and away from the camera, quickly becomes a blur. She seems to be fleeing the German milieu and the world of the film as rapidly as decency will allow, and the filmmakers assist her in departing from the film's field of vision. Petzold knows that Nelly cannot get out of there fast enough, and he thus accelerates the process by which she drops out of sight, moving away from Johnny and toward a brighter light. The shift in focus suggests that Johnny may be straining to understand what he missed, but that his effort comes too late. She was next to him all along and is now whisking herself away. As with Orpheus, who was told that he could not descend into the netherworld for a second time, Johnny will not receive another chance.

Choosing not to depict or even hint at the idea that Nelly might emigrate to Palestine, Petzold's film travels no further with her. This last shot is from Johnny's point of view, as he finds himself pinned to the piano bench, prohibited from following. She offers him no reconciliation. *Schindler's List* ended with a redemptive sequence, highlighting a trajectory from the tragedy of the Holocaust to the establishment of Israel. Although Petzold and Farocki's screenplay introduces a series of discussions about whether or not Nelly should leave Germany behind, we never come to know whether anything like this happens. All we know for certain is that for them—for Johnny

Nelly, no longer in focus, exits the room.

and Nelly, the once harmoniously bonded German and German Jew—there will be, to use Lene's phrase, no moving forward.

Writing in 1950, Arendt argued that there was an almost instinctive urge among Germans "to take refuge in the thoughts and ideas one held before anything compromising had happened. The result is that while Germany has changed beyond recognition—physically and psychologically—people talk and behave superficially as though absolutely nothing had happened since 1932."[92] Moses Moskowitz, who represented the Foreign Affairs Division of the American Jewish Committee, wrote in 1946 that most of the remaining Jews in Germany had decided to emigrate because they perceived no inclination on the part of Germans to make amends for the crimes of Nazism. He adds the philosophical remark that for persons incapable of realizing errors, "there is no hope."[93] The hope in *Phoenix* lies in its open acknowledgment that postwar German film, fascinating as it was, was also complicit in avoiding accountability. For this reason Petzold and Farocki dig through film history's ruins with the intention of extending otherwise abandoned histories and traditions. If *Phoenix* is a reckoning with German ghosts and with cinema's gaps, then it is also a séance in which the contributions of no small number of artists, émigrés, and victims are given voice.

CREDITS

Director:
Christian Petzold

Assistant Director:
Ires Jung

Writers:
Christian Petzold (author)
Harun Farocki (co-author)
Based on the novel *Le retour des cendres* by
    Hubert Monteilhet

Production Companies:
Schramm Film Koerner & Weber
Tempus Film
BR/ WDR/ Arte

Produced by:
Florian Koerner von Gustorf
Michael Weber

Cast:
Nina Hoss as Nelly Lenz
Ronald Zehrfeld as Johnny Lenz
Nina Kunzendorf as Lene Winter
Imogen Kogge as Elisabeth

Music:
Stefan Will

Cinematography:
Hans Fromm

Film Editing:
Bettina Böhler

Costume Design:
Anette Guther

Release Dates:
World premiere: September 5, 2014 at the
    Toronto International Film Festival
German theatrical premiere: September 25,
    2014

Runtime:
1 hr., 34 min.

Sound Mix:
Dolby Digital

Aspect Ratio:
2.39: 1

Camera:
Leica Summilux-C Lenses

Negative Format:
35 mm

Cinematographic Process:
Super 35

Printed Film Format:
DCP

Locations:
Phoenix was filmed between August and
    October 2013 in Brandenburg, Germany
    and in Legnica and Wrocław in Poland.

NOTES

1   According to Petzold, "[Farocki] said we have to start *Phoenix* in the night, like in *The Killers*." See Daniel Kasman, "Filming Around the Wound: A Conversation with Christian Petzold." *mubi.com*, https://mubi.com/notebook/posts/filming-around-the-wound-a-conversation-with-christian-petzold.

2   See Neil Young, "The Past Is Not Myself," *Sight & Sound* 25, no. 6 (June 2015): 38–41; here 40.

3   See Young, "The Past Is Not Myself," 40.

4   Petzold says, "[*Phoenix*] is a film noir! Fassbinder needed the Douglas Sirk films to make his period pictures, and I need film noir to make mine." See Nicolas Rapold, "Interview: Christian Petzold," *filmcomment.com*, February 26, 2015, https://www.filmcomment.com/blog/interview-christian-petzold/.

5   See Theodor Adorno, *Minima Moralia: Reflections from Damaged Life* (London: Verso, 1974, 1985), 33.

6   Gerd Gemünden, *Continental Strangers: German Exile Cinema, 1933–1951* (New York: Columbia University Press, 2014), 4.

7   Lutz Koepnick, *The Dark Mirror: German Cinema between Hitler and Hollywood* (Berkeley and Los Angeles: University of California, 2002), 159.

8   For Farocki's analysis of *The Phantom Lady*, see his "Vertauschte Frauen" in *Filmkritik* 282 (1980, no. 6): 274–79.

9   Weill was Jewish, Lenya was not. For Petzold's comment, see Frank Arnold, "Die Historie muss ein Geheimnis bleiben: Christian Petzold über seinen Film *Phoenix*," *epd-film.de*, Sept. 25, 2014, https://www.epd-film.de/meldungen/2014/die-historie-muss-ein-geheimnis-bleiben.

10 On connections between *Jerichow* and Fassbinder's films, see Jaimey Fisher, *Christian Petzold* (Urbana, IL: University of Illinois Press, 2013), 126 and 128.

11 In his interview with Young ("The Past Is Not Myself"), Petzold explains that he is unfamiliar with Thompson's 1965 film and that he read Monteilhet's novel in German in the 1980s (40).

12 Farocki himself was a student at the DFFB from 1966 to 1968. On the earliest phase of his influence on Petzold, see Marco Abel, "'Das ist vorbei': Untimely Encounters with Neoliberalism in Christian Petzold's dffb Student Films," *Senses of Cinema* 84 (September 2017), http://sensesofcinema.com/2017/christian-petzold-a-dossier/christian-petzold-student-films/.

13 See Fisher's interview with Petzold in Fisher, *Christian Petzold*, 151.

14 Mentioned in Fisher, *Christian Petzold*, 151.

15 In his interview with Young ("The Past Is Not Myself"), Petzold says that he and Farocki planned to watch the film in the middle of August, but shortly before then, Farocki had a heart attack and died. "He never saw the film. But we talked about this film for, I think, 15 years" (41).

16 After so many years of Bauer not being on the radar, it is noteworthy that in the span of two or three years there have been several films that directly or indirectly reference him. For a sharply critical assessment of *Labyrinth of Lies*, see Nora Bierich, "Zur väterlichen Nebenrolle degradiert—*Im Labyrinth des Schweigens*. Ein Film über und ohne Fritz Bauer," zeitgeschichte-online.de, https://zeitgeschichte-online.de/film/zur-vaeterlichen-nebenrolle-degradiert-im-labyrinth-des-schweigens.

17 Bauer found himself in trouble when, in 1963 he remarked to a Danish newspaper that anti-Semitism persisted in Germany and explained that Germans nowadays no longer malign Jews as swine, but rather tell them, "We forgot to gas you" (*Wir haben vergessen, dich zu vergasen*). See Ronen Steinke, "Der Vorwurf der Befangenheit: Fritz Bauer in den Interview-Affären 1963 und 1965," in *Rückkehr in Feindesland? Fritz Bauer in der deutsch-jüdischen Nachkriegsgeschichte*, ed. Katharina Rauschenberger (Frankfurt and New York: Campus Verlag, 2013), 122. The interview was with the Danish tabloid *B. T.* (an edition of *Berlingske Tidende*) in February 1963.

18 Marco Abel, *The Counter-Cinema of the Berlin School* (Rochester, NY: Camden House, 2015), 72.

19 Marco Abel, "The Cinema of Identification Gets on my Nerves: An Interview with Christian Petzold," *Cineaste Magazine* 33.3 (2008), https://www.cineaste.com/summer2008/the-cinema-of-identification-gets-on-my-nerves/.

20 Abel, "The Cinema of Identification." According to Petzold, Monteilhet's novel inspired him to think of how little *Heimkehrer* literature in the German language dealt with camp survivors and displaced persons. See Peter Osteried, "Interview mit Christian Petzold über Phoenix," *kritiken.de*, Aug. 26, 2014. https://www.kritiken.de/interview/christian-petzold-ueber-phoenix-26-08-2014.html.

21 See Walter Jens, *Moderne Literatur, Moderne Wirklichkeit* (Pfullingen: Günther Neske, 1959), 19.

22 In *Invisible Agent* (1941), the Invisible Man's face was not bandaged, but rather masked.

23 See Rapold, "Interview: Christian Petzold," n.p.

24 J. Hoberman concludes, "In Petzold's appreciation for Hollywood tropes, as well as his sensitivity to historical setting, he is Fassbinder's most credible heir." See "The Waiting Rooms of History," *The New York Review of Books*, March 7, 2019, 20–22; here 22.

25 Concerning this point, see the description of the same scene in Olivia Landry, *Movement and Performance in Berlin School Cinema* (Bloomington: Indiana University Press, 2018), 173.

26 Corina Erk observes that Nelly's unbandaged face remains unseen for well over 10 minutes. She writes, "The camera does not provide a view of Nelly's disfigured face [...] because Petzold's film as a whole refuses to provide a voyeuristic view of a concentration

camp victim's scars, and thereby refuses to show the horrors of the camps. It turns away just as the US soldier turns away. The horror of the camp [...] emerges instead through the refusal of images." See Erk, "'Ich stelle mich auf die Seite der Gespenster.' Grauen und Geister in Christian Petzolds *Phoenix*," in *Ordnungen des Unheimlichen. Kultur—Literatur—Medien*, ed. Florian Lehmann (Würzburg: Königshausen & Neumann 2016), 311–21; here, 314. My translation.

27 Primo Levi, *The Drowned and the Saved*, trans. Raymond Rosenthal (New York: Vintage, 1989 [orig. 1986]), 75.

28 Atina Grossmann, "Where Did All 'Our' Jews Go? Germans and Jews in Post-Nazi Germany," in *The Germans and the Holocaust: Popular Responses to the Persecution and Murder of the Jews*, ed. Susanna Schrafstetter and Alan E. Steinweis (New York: Berghahn, 2016), 131–54; here 131.

29 Grossmann, "Where Did All 'Our' Jews Go?," 143.

30 Ruth Gay, *Safe Among the Germans: Liberated Jews after World War II* (New Haven: Yale University Press, 2002), 146–47. Similar numbers are shown in *Jüdische Geschichte in Berlin: Bilder und Dokumente*, vol. 1, ed. Reinhard Rürup (Berlin: Edition Hentrich, 1995), 336, as well as in Eva Kolinsky, *After the Holocaust: Jewish Survivors in Germany after 1945* (London: Pimlico, 2004), 135.

31 Hubert Monteilhet, *Return from the Ashes*, trans. Richard Howard (New York: Signet, 1963 [orig. 1961]), 10; for de Hair's German translation, see the Rororo Thriller edition, which collects three criminal novels: *Ich bin ein anderer/ Der Asche entstiegen/ Sieben Tage Frist für Schramm* (Reinbek: Rowohlt, 1981), 272.

32 See Mauriac's foreword to Elie Wiesel, *Night* (New York: Hill and Wang, 2006 [orig. 1958]), n.p. See also Mauthausen survivor Jean Cayrol's *Lazare parmi nous* (1950), which appeared in German as *Lazarus unter uns*, trans. Sigrid von Massenbach (Stuttgart: Schwab, 1959).

33 In his interview with Young ("The Past Is Not Myself"), Petzold says, "The Germans after the war kept talking about 'zero,' our 'Year Zero'—they are the 'phoenix,' I think. They said, 'Everything is destroyed, now we are stronger than before.' This is the phoenix myth, I think. This is why the film has the title 'Phoenix'—it's not Nelly. Nelly is no phoenix" (41).

34 Monteilhet, *Return from the Ashes*, 38; *Der Asche entstiegen*, 295.

35 Walter Benjamin, "Theses on the Philosophy of History," in *Illuminations*, ed. Hannah Arendt, trans. Harry Zohn (New York: Schocken, 1955), 257–58.

36 Benjamin, "Theses on the Philosophy of History," 257.

37 One film in which this theme is developed is Hiroshi Teshigahara's *The Face of Another* (*Tanin no kao*, 1966).

38 Monteilhet, *Return from the Ashes*, 15. Petzold refers to this scene in the interview with Young. See "The Past Is Not Myself," 40.

39 Monteilhet, *Return from the Ashes*, 15.

40 See Gemünden, "Die Masken des Bösen: Peter Lorre im Exil," in *Peter Lorre: Ein Fremder im Paradies*, ed. Michael Omasta, Brigitte Mayr, and Elisabeth Streit (Vienna: Zsolnay, 2004), 110–22; here, 121.

41 Petzold discusses Farocki's essay film in Kasman, "Filming Around the Wound."

42 Christian Petzold, "The Face Behind the Mask," in *Peter Lorre: Ein Fremder im Paradies*, 123–27.

43 Petzold says, "[*The Face Behind the Mask*] is a very fantastic movie. I showed it to the art director, our hospital was completely stolen from that!" See Kasman, "Filming Around the Wound."

44 See Hannah Steinhoff, "Ich mag keine Nazis ins Bild setzen," *planet-interview.de*, September 29, 2014, http://www.planet-interview.de/interviews/christian-petzold/46231/.

45 See Michael Cieply, "Hollywood Production: An Honorary Oscar Revives a Controversy," *New York Times*, Nov. 1, 2010, A1. https://www.nytimes.com/2010/11/02/movies/02godard.html.

46 For an example of this position, see Dietrich Kuhlbrodt, *Deutsches Filmwunder: Nazis immer besser* (Hamburg: Konkret Literatur Verlag, 2006).

47 Petzold describes the first day's shooting of *Phoenix*: "I fell into the trap of the scenery: a forest, a woman is shot, a Russian jeep drives by … I realized that this is exactly the crap I didn't want. And not for aesthetic, but for moral reasons […]. I could not just stage an extermination and pretend that everything was possible! […] It was really good to throw away the material from the first day of shooting. Incidentally, I have thrown away the material from the first day of shooting in all my films! Maybe you have to do it wrong on the first day so that you can find the right, unique tone for a new movie." See Anke Westphal, "Interview mit Christian Petzold über *Phoenix* 'Ich wollte kein Guido-Knopp-TV,'" *berliner-zeitung.de*, Sept. 8, 2014, https://www.berliner-zeitung.de/kultur/interview-mit-christian-petzold-ueber--phoenix---ich-wollte-kein-guido-knopp-tv--224750. My translation.

48 See Nayman, "The Face of Another: Christian Petzold's *Phoenix*," *cinema-scope.com*, December 2014, http://cinema-scope.com/features/face-another-christian-petzolds-phoenix/. In his interview with Young ("The Past Is Not Myself"), Petzold says, "when I shot it, I felt embarrassed, ashamed, because I had done the same thing that all the other Holocaust movies do. They think they can make pictures of the Holocaust, and that's not possible. I don't like *The Boy in the Striped Pyjamas* (2008), films like that. So I cut it out—I used part of it later for a brief dream sequence" (40).

49 The information about *Yella* and Hitchcock's *Marnie* appears in Nayman, "Face of Another."

50 Claude Lanzmann, "Seminar with Claude Lanzmann 11 April 1990," *Yale French Studies* 79 (1991): 82–99; here, 96.

51 See, for example, Lanzmann's "Holocaust, die unmögliche Darstellung. Zu *Schindlers Liste*," in *Das Grab des göttlichen Tauchers: Ausgewählte Texte*, trans. Erich Wolfgang Skwara (Reinbek: Rowohlt, 2015 [orig. 1994]), 492–98.

52 The characters are interlinked: their names, Nelly and Yella, share a nearly anagrammatic relationship—to say nothing of Leyla, the character played by Hoss in Petzold's 2001 film *Something to Remind Me* (*Toter Mann*), a thriller that was also, in part, inspired by *Vertigo*. Petzold confirms the intentionality of the interconnection between Nelly and Yella's names in "'Ein Raum, in dem wir heimisch sind': Interview mit Christian Petzold," *Über Christian Petzold*, ed. Ilke Brombach and Tina Kaiser (Berlin: Vorwerk 8, 2018), 19–60; here, 52.

53 See Erk ("Ich stelle mich auf die Seite der Gespenster"), who discusses the shudder [*Schauder*] in connection with Lene's character. Erk writes "The horror Lene faces daily during her work in the Agency does not produce a cathartic effect, but instead causes a constant shudder [*ein konstantes Schaudern*] in her life, as a result of which she chooses suicide" (315; my translation). See also the description of Lene in Petzold's interview with Peter Osteried, "Interview mit Christian Petzold über Phoenix," August 26, 2014, *kritiken.de* https://www.kritiken.de/interview/christian-petzold-ueber-phoenix-26-08-2014.html.

54 Petzold says that *The Murderers Are Among Us* was the only rubble film he looked at while he was making *Phoenix*. See Jaimey Fisher and Robert Fischer, "The Cinema is a Warehouse of Memory: A Conversation Among Christian Petzold, Robert Fischer, and Jaimey Fisher," *Senses of Cinema* 84, September 2017, http://sensesofcinema.com/2017/christian-petzold-a-dossier/christian-petzold/.

55 See Nelly Sachs, "Chorus of the Rescued," trans. Michael Roloff, *Collected Poems: 1944–1949* (Los Angeles: Green Integer, 2011), 101–3.

56 On Sachs's reluctance to reconcile, see especially Katja Garloff's chapter in Garloff, *Words from Abroad: Trauma and Displacement in Postwar German Jewish Writers* (Detroit: Wayne State University Press, 2005), 95–130.

57 See Jennifer Fay and Justus Nieland, *Film Noir: Hard-Boiled Modernity and the Cultures of Globalization* (London and New York: Routledge, 2010), 46–47.

58 *Phoenix* is not the only film of Petzold's that thematizes lesbian desire. See Joy Castro, "'A Place without Parents': Queer and Maternal Desire in the Films of Christian Petzold," *Senses of Cinema* 84 (2017). http://sensesofcinema.com/2017/christian-petzold-a-dossier/queer-and-maternal-desire-christian-petzold/.

59 Foster Hirsch, *Kurt Weill on Stage: From Berlin to Broadway* (New York: Limelight Editions, 2003), 219.

60 Hirsch, *Kurt Weill on Stage*, 219.

61 The similarity is discussed by Jaimey Fisher in "Petzold's *Phoenix*, Fassbinder's *Maria Braun*, and the Melodramatic Archaeology of the Rubble Past," *Senses of Cinema* 84, September 2017. http://sensesofcinema.com/2017/christian-petzold-a-dossier/petzold-fassbinder/.

62 Monteilhet, *Return from the Ashes*, 23; *Der Asche entstiegen*, 282.

63 Paul W. Massing and Maxwell Miller, "Should Jews Return to Germany?" *The Atlantic Monthly* 176 (July 1945), 87–90; here 88.

64 Massing and Miller, "Should Jews Return to Germany?," 90.

65 Hannah Arendt, "The Aftermath of Nazi Rule," *Commentary* 10, no. 4 (October 1950): 342–53: here 342.

66 Petzold discusses the cabaret culture in Susanne Burg, "'Ich hasse allegorische Filme': Regisseur Petzold über seinen neuen Film *Phoenix*," *deutschlandfunkkultur.de*, Sept. 20, 2014. https://www.deutschlandfunkkultur.de/christian-petzold-ich-hasse-allegorische-filme.2168.de.html?dram:article_id=298099.

67 Peter Kummel, "Nelly kehrt heim," *Die Zeit* 39 (October 6, 2014). https://www.zeit.de/2014/39/phoenix-christian-petzold.

68 In the other major critical review of *Phoenix* to be published in Germany, Georg Diez writes that he is surprised that no one involved with the production realized that the premise that Lene has a nice apartment with a housekeeper while Germans are starving in the ruins confirms an anti-Semitic trope. See Diez, "Was soll das?" *Der Spiegel* 39 (2014): 127.

69 Malte Hagener notes that Petzold has more than once mentioned his longstanding interest in *Vertigo*. See "Konzentrische Kreise: Filmgeschichte als Matrix im Werk von Christian Petzold," *Über Christian Petzold*, 159–71; here, 160.

70 Chris Marker takes note of Kim Novak's red dressing gown. See Marker, "A Free Replay (Notes on *Vertigo*)," 4. https://chrismarker.org/chris-marker/a-free-replay-notes-on-vertigo/. Marker's essay was originally published in French in *Positif* 400 (June 1994): 79–84.

71 Gemünden, *Continental Strangers*, 6.

72 Hannah Arendt, "We Refugees," in *Altogether Elsewhere: Writers on Exile*, ed. Marc Robinson (Boston: Faber and Faber, 1994 [orig. 1943]), 110–19; here, 111.

73 Arendt, "We Refugees," 111.

74 Harun Farocki, "Vertauschte Frauen." See also Petzold's references to this essay in *Ray Magazine*. http://www.ray-magazin.at/magazin/2007/12/dossier-yella-christian-petzold-im-gespraech. See also Arnold, "Die Historie muss ein Geheimnis bleiben," in which Petzold again mentions Farocki's essay.

75 Farocki, "Vertauschte Frauen," 276. Farocki uses Woolrich's pseudonym William Irish. See also Petzold's discussion of Siodmak's *Phantom Lady* in Kasman, "Filming Around the Wound."

76 See Young, "The Past Is Not Myself," 40.

77 Farocki, "Vertauschte Frauen," 276.

78 Petzold says, "It's impossible to go back, because everything has changed. You see in the last travelling shot in *Nuit et brouillard* (*Night and Fog*) a barber's chair, and it's just a chair,

but it now seems like the most horrible torture implement you've ever seen in your life."
See Nayman, "The Face of Another."

79 In the German translation of Monteilhet: "Eifersüchtig! Und auf mich selbst!" (*Der Asche Entstiegen*, 285). See also *Return from the Ashes*, 26.

80 Jean Amèry, "Resentments," in *At the Mind's Limits: Contemplations by a Survivor on Auschwitz and Its Realities*, trans. Sydney Rosenfeld and Stella P. Rosenfeld (Bloomington: Indiana University Press, 1980 [orig. 1966]), 62–81; esp. 67.

81 Petzold says that pairing Hoss and Zehrfeld in another film was Farocki's suggestion. See "Ein Raum, in dem wir heimisch sind," in *Über Christian Petzold*, 50.

82 Petzold says that, for the audio mix in this scene, he drew inspiration from a similar scene in Yasujirô Ozu's postwar drama *Late Spring* (1949). See Kasman, "Filming Around the Wound."

83 See Marker, "A Free Replay," 5.

84 In *Return from the Ashes*, Stanislas proposes that Elizabeth give herself a camp tattoo. See Monteilhet, 49.

85 Levi, *The Drowned and the Saved*, 119.

86 Levi, *The Drowned and the Saved*, 119–20.

87 Dora Apel, "The Tattooed Jew," in *Visual Culture and the Holocaust*, ed. Barbie Zelizer (New Brunswick, NJ: Rutgers University Press, 2001) 300–320; here 302.

88 See Kasman, "Filming Around the Wound."

89 The phenomenon is discussed by Adorno and by Peter Schönbach. See Schönbach, *Reaktionen auf die antisemitische Welle im Winter 1959/1960* (Frankfurt a.M: Europäische Verlagsanstalt, 1961), which Adorno assisted in writing. For a thorough definition of secondary anti-Semitism, see Evelien Gans, "'They Have Forgotten to Gas You': Post-1945 Antisemitism in the Netherlands, in *Dutch Racism* (Leiden: Brill, 2014), 71–100; here, 84–90.

90 Hans-Jürgen Schaal refers to the song's "quasi-parlando" in "Speak Low," *Jazz-Standards: Das Lexikon* (Kassel: Bärenreiter, 2001), 452–53; here 453.

91 On the contrast between Johnny's blank stare and Nelly's turn away from the camera in the film's final moments, see Tina Kaiser, "'Darling, It's Late': Notizen zum abgewandten Gesicht in *Phoenix*," *Über Christian Petzold*, 213–21; here, 219.

92 Arendt, "The Aftermath of Nazi Rule," 344.

93 Moses Moskowitz, "The Germans and the Jews: Postwar Report. The Enigma of German Irresponsibility," *Commentary* 2, no. 1 (July 1946): 7–14; here 13.